The Nuclear Future

CORNELL STUDIES IN
SECURITY AFFAIRS

edited by Robert J. Art
and Robert Jervis

John J. Mearsheimer, *Conventional Deterrence*
Michael Mandelbaum, *The Nuclear Future*

ALSO BY MICHAEL MANDELBAUM:

*The Nuclear Question: The United States and Nuclear Weapons,
1946–1976* (1979)

*The Nuclear Revolution: International Politics Before and After Hiro-
shima* (1981)

The Nuclear Future

MICHAEL MANDELBAUM

Cornell University Press

ITHACA AND LONDON

First published 1983 by Cornell University Press.
Published in the United Kingdom by Cornell University Press, Ltd., London.

International Standard Book Number (cloth) 0–8014–1619–1
International Standard Book Number (paper) 0–8014–9254–8
Library of Congress Catalog Card Number 82-74068
Printed in the United States of America
Librarians: Library of Congress cataloging information appears on the last page of the book.

To my wife,
Anne Mandelbaum,
with love

Contents

[7]

Preface

The Nuclear Future is designed to enable the general reader to understand the ongoing debate about nuclear weapons and to evaluate the dangers that they pose. The book describes the world's present nuclear state: the main scientific and technical features of the weapons in existence, the various types of weapons, and the political doctrines that govern them.

Chapter 1 offers an overview of the world's nuclear arrangements. Chapter 2 gives special attention to the nuclear arsenals of the United States and the Soviet Union and to the relationship between the superpowers. Chapter 3 is devoted to something that has received comparatively little attention in the recent controversies but that may represent the greatest threat to our safety: the spread of nuclear weapons to countries that do not now have them. Chapter 4 discusses the anti–nuclear weapons movements that have arisen in both the United States and Western Europe over the last few years. Chapter 5 offers some predictions about the future of nuclear weapons. The predictions have a common theme: that the future will be much like the past; that the world will neither rid itself of these weapons altogether nor be consumed by a vast nuclear holocaust between now and the year 2000.

At the end of the book the reader will find a list of other works on nuclear weapons and a glossary of some of the special terms that are common in writings about the subject.

The Nuclear Future began as a paper for a conference at the Naval War College in Newport, Rhode Island, on the subject "Security Policy in an Insecure Age." The original paper was published as "The Future of Nuclear Weapons" in the September–October 1982 issue of the *Naval War College Review*. I am grateful to Robert Murray, director of the War College's Center for Naval Warfare Studies, and to Thomas Etzold, the Center's Director of Strategic Research, for commissioning the original paper and giving permission to expand it to book length.

In writing the book I received extraordinarily valuable advice from David Freeman, Robert Jervis, Walter H. Lippincott, Jr., Anne Mandelbaum, Strobe Talbott, and Richard H. Ullman.

I enjoyed the use of the facilities of the Research Institute on International Change at Columbia University, and am happy to express my appreciation to the Institute's director, Seweryn Bialer, for his courtesy.

I presented an excerpt from the book to a seminar at the Lehrman Institute of New York City. I am grateful to Nicholas X. Rizopoulos, executive director of the Institute, and to the members of the seminar for helpful suggestions.

The book was completed before but is being published during my term as an International Affairs Fellow of the Council on Foreign Relations of New York City at the

Preface

Department of State. The views expressed are my own
and not those of either institution.

MICHAEL MANDELBAUM

Washington, D.C.

The Nuclear Future

[1]

The Nuclear Future

Almost forty years after it began, the nuclear age has entered a crisis of middle life. In August 1945 the United States destroyed the Japanese cities of Hiroshima and Nagasaki, each by a single explosion that drew its power from the energy locked in the heart of matter. Twenty-five years later the United States and the Soviet Union had accumulated enough nuclear weapons to perpetrate a thousand Hiroshimas in a single afternoon. Now each could, if it chose to do so, turn a whole country, conceivably the whole world, into a Hiroshima. Yet for most of the period since 1945, the world has lived with reasonable comfort, or at least with only occasionally evident discomfort, with the bomb. And the periodic outbursts of anxiety of the 1940s and 1950s gave way, after 1963, to almost two decades in which nuclear weapons, for all their power and the dangers they posed, remained far from the forefront of public concern. They were out of sight—few were located near population centers; many were placed underground or undersea—and so very nearly out of mind.

Of course, "the Bomb" surfaced in most people's thoughts from time to time, and nuclear weapons became the full-time preoccupation of a small group of people. The number of Americans who have designed, stood guard over, and worked out the rules for deploying and using—or threatening to use—these armaments probably does not exceed the hundreds of thousands. The number with direct nuclear responsibilities in the Soviet Union has probably been smaller; in Western Europe it has certainly been much smaller. The future of the world depends on nuclear weapons in the sense that they could destroy much of what is living on the planet; but only a tiny fraction of the world's population has ever had anything directly to do with them.

The nuclear experts are similar to the priests of traditional societies, whose role it was to serve as intermediaries between ordinary people and the gods. It is through their nuclear-weapon specialists that industrial societies are connected with the most powerful of all earthly forces. The nuclear priesthood is not the precise equivalent of the Hindu Brahmins or the Levites of ancient Israel. It is not a closed caste, and membership is not hereditary. The custodian of the nuclear arsenal of the United States, the American president, is elected by popular vote. With their specialized vocabulary and body of technical information, nuclear-weapon specialists are like other cadres of experts in modern society—doctors, lawyers, scientists, engineers. None of these other groups, however, has responsibility for anything so powerful yet so abstract.

In the early 1980s the public in the West appeared to be bent on wresting control of nuclear weapons from the government officials, military officers, and private specialists who comprise the nuclear priesthood. At any given moment in Western societies a public conversation is always under way on some topic that engages the country as a whole rather than a few experts; it takes place in the chambers of public bodies and private associations, on television and radio and in newspapers and periodicals, and in private discussions. Over the last twenty years the condition of the national economy and, in the United States, race relations and the Vietnam war were the most important topics.

In the spring of 1982, nuclear weapons assumed the place that these subjects had once held. There was an outpouring of books, articles, and television programs on the subject. It became an issue around which citizens organized themselves. It inspired marches, rallies, petitions, and ultimately legislation. The fate of the earth, to use the title of the most widely read of the books about nuclear weapons, suddenly seemed too important to be left to the experts. Americans and Europeans as a whole had become preoccupied with the nuclear future.

They were preoccupied with two radically different nuclear futures. There was mounting concern about nuclear war. Books appeared telling how such a conflict might begin. The origins of World War III provided fertile gound for imaginative speculation. A variety of sequences of events—"scenarios" is the word often used for them—have been proposed: distant countries going to war and drawing others in; madmen getting control of bombs; complicated pieces of machinery malfunctioning. All such scenarios end in catastrophe. A series of television programs showed what a nuclear attack would do to a community, putting to use the skills at simulating destruction that have been developed for disaster movies.

At the same time a prominent theme of the public conversation was nuclear disarmament. There was a yearning for a world that was free of the danger of nuclear war because it was free of the weapons with which such a war would be fought. The hope for this second nuclear future is a natural response to the fear of the first one. Little was said about how it might come about. Nuclear disarmament was less a political program than a simple, deeply felt demand, a demand based on the view that so monstrous a threat required a total remedy.

Nuclear war and nuclear disarmament are the worst and best of all nuclear futures. They are polar opposites— the inferno and paradise. They are also limiting cases. Each would solve the problem that the existence of nuclear weapons presents, although in quite different ways: disarmament would remove the danger of catastrophe, leaving the world to struggle with the afflictions with which it had to contend before 1945. After a nuclear war there might well be no future about which to be concerned.

Nuclear war and nuclear disarmament have something else in common. Neither is a likely nuclear future.

Nuclear disarmament is unlikely because it would require a radical change in the way international politics is organized, a change for which there is no clear precedent in 2,500 years of recorded history and which is not at all likely to take place in our own day. The term for the way the system of sovereign nations, the basic units of international politics, is structured is "anarchy." Anarchy does not mean chaos but rather the absence of formal order; that is, the absence of government. The world's sovereign countries, which belong to the United Nations and sign treaties with each other, have a variety of institutions and powers. Most important, they have armed forces and the power to go to war.

There is no global authority to stop them. No world

government exists to guide and regulate their relations with each other. The international system has nothing comparable to the governments *within* countries, with their police and courts. There is a world parliament of sorts, in the form of the United Nations General Assembly, and a World Court, which is associated with the U.N. No military force stands behind them, however. Their edicts are purely advisory, and are routinely ignored.

Anarchy is the root of the problem of nuclear weapons. Countries will worry that their neighbors will attack them as long as there is nothing to prevent the neighbors from doing so. They will feel the need to be prepared for attacks, and to discourage them if possible, by having armaments. In societies without law, as on the American frontier in the nineteenth century, citizens tend to form vigilante groups to protect themselves. The world of sovereign states is such a society, and each state is a vigilante. This is the case even when no outlaw is visible. Every state wants to be prepared in case one comes along. It is the anarchic character of the international system, not the wickedness or belligerence of any particular member of it, that is the basic reason countries believe they must have weapons. The most powerful countries invariably have the most powerful weapons. In our own day these weapons are nuclear.

Even if there were a world government, complete nuclear disarmament might not be possible; such a government might well need to have nuclear weapons to enforce its decisions. But world government is not in the offing. As the necessary precondition for disarmament and therefore the way to put an end to the ancient scourge of war, it is a compelling idea. It has often been suggested, and most often in the nuclear age. Many of the proposals for controlling nuclear weapons in the years immediately after World War II, beginning with the American-sponsored Baruch Plan of 1946, called for the establishment of a powerful supranational authority; some people explicitly envisioned a global body with full governmental powers. None of these proposals came close to being adopted. Countries do not want to give up their sovereign prerogatives, especially the most basic one of all, that of going to war.

In the contemporary period, in fact, the trend is in the opposite direction. The world has seen the multiplication, or perhaps more accurately the division, of sovereignty, not its restriction and consolidation. Almost every national or linguistic group now wants its own sovereign state, with all the trappings. Many have gained it. There are many more independent countries now than there were at the beginning of the century. Then much of the world was parceled out among multinational empires that had been pieced together by the great powers of Europe. Those empires broke apart, leaving many sovereign states in their wake.

The nations of the world could conceivably renounce nuclear weapons. They could agree to go about their business, including their quarrels with each other, without having these armaments. Nothing of the sort has happened so far, nor is it likely to happen in the future. The difficulty goes back to the anarchy of the international system. Renunciation would mean that each country trusted the others not to have, or to get, nuclear weapons. Complete trust is unlikely, however, when the possibility exists that others *could* get them, and when no governing authority could prevent them from doing so.

[20]

Even if every sovereign state promised not to have nuclear weapons, moreover, this vow would not make for an entirely nuclear-free world. It would, rather, be a world separated from nuclear weapons by the time it would take to make them. The knowledge of how to make them would remain. It could not be readily forgotten, as the learning of antiquity was largely forgotten in the Middle Ages. To root it out would require not just forgetting the formula for designing bombs but, since the weapons are based on the fundamental laws of physics, abolishing human inquiry into the workings of the physical universe.

The movement of history and the evolution of culture that produced nuclear weapons are irreversible. The atomic physicists, acting for all of us, bit into the apple of knowledge. A return to prenuclear innocence is no more possible for humankind in the twentieth century than a return to the Garden of Eden was for Adam and Eve. Nuclear weapons are the product of the two most powerful social forces of the twentieth century—nationalism and science. A world without them would bear no resemblance to the one in which we live. Nuclear disarmament would require their abolition. It would require a revolution in human affairs more sweeping than anything that has happened in this century or is to be expected in the next. The abolition of all nuclear weapons is not simply formidably difficult to achieve. It is difficult even to imagine.

Nuclear war can be and has been all too readily imagined. It is, however, not more but rather less likely to occur for that reason. The world is well aware that as long as the weapons exist, it will be possible to use them. It is aware that the result of their use would be disaster.

[21]

This awareness has tempered the foreign policies of the owners of these weapons with caution, especially in their relations with each other. The types of events that make up the scenarios of nuclear war have already occurred. There *have* been wars in which countries with nuclear weapons have taken part, directly and indirectly. None has turned into a nuclear war. This circumstance has been the result neither of accident nor of luck, at least not entirely. International conflicts have stopped short of becoming nuclear because the countries that have fought them have been at pains to limit them in this way.

Not only have the world's leaders behaved cautiously when the use of nuclear weapons seemed possible, they have actually said that their caution was induced by the dangers these weapons present. All nations that have them say that their nuclear weapons are for defensive purposes only—that they have them, in fact, not to use them against others but to prevent others from making nuclear attacks against them.

They are not the first countries to say this sort of thing, however, nor are nuclear weapons the first armaments for which purely defensive intentions have been proclaimed. Powerful new weapons have appeared in the past, making war more destructive than it was before. All such weapons—artillery, cannon, poison gas, napalm, and all the rest—have been used at some point. Nuclear weapons constitute the third, not the first, revolutionary advance in military power in modern times. All three advances took place in the midst of ongoing wars, when it seemed natural, indeed imperative, to use the new techniques of violence. The first modern military revolution, the mobilization of an entire society for war—which, combined with the use of offensive tactics on the battlefield, made Napoleon's armies masters of Europe—came during the wars of the French Revolution. The second, the systematic union of industrialism and warfare, which brought the machine gun and ultimately the tank and the airplane into common use in war, occurred during World War I. The Manhattan Project, which produced the first atomic bombs, began while World War II was under way. Since 1945 the world has had the opportunity to absorb the lessons of Hiroshima and Nagasaki, to learn how powerful and dangerous nuclear weapons are; and the world's supply of nuclear weapons has become much more powerful and dangerous since 1945 than it was then.

Of course the memory of Austerlitz did not prevent World War I, or the memory of Verdun World War II. The nuclear revolution, however, is different. Nuclear weapons can kill more people and lay waste to more property than any other armaments. They are weapons of mass destruction. The difference in destructive power between nuclear and all other weapons is not just a matter of degree. These weapons are not just the furthest point of the linear extension of military force, from stones through gunpowder to high explosives of various chemical compositions. Other weapons could in theory do much of what nuclear weapons can do. The difference is, as the economist and strategic thinker Thomas C. Schelling has noted, that "nuclear weapons can do it quickly." "To compress a catastrophic war within the span of time that a man can stay awake," he has written, "drastically changes the politics of war, the process of decision, the possibility of central control and restraint, the motivations of the people in charge, and the capacity to think and reflect while war is in progress. It is imagin-

able that we might destroy 200,000,000 Russians in a war
of the present, although not 80,000,000 Japanese in a
war of the past. It is not only imaginable, it is imagined.
It is imagined because it could be done in a moment, in
the twinkling of an eye, at the last trumpet." That is,
nuclear weapons are so powerful that it is questionable
whether the destruction in a war in which they were
used could be kept short of levels that no political goals
could justify.

A nuclear war would destroy not only lives but in all
likelihood a way of life. Modern societies are not com-
posed of isolated groups of people in autonomous settle-
ments, but of networks that knit them together on a large
scale. The citizens of modern societies do not rely on
themselves for food, water, shelter, and transportation.
They depend on millions of others. Nuclear war would
shatter the networks that support modern existence.

It poses an even greater threat—not only to our modern
way of life, but to life itself. It might alter not only the
social but the natural environment. The climate, the soil,
the atmosphere that shields living things from the full
force of the sun's rays might all be damaged. A particular combination of conditions makes life possible on the
planet earth. Nuclear war, unlike any war of the past,
could change those conditions.

These potential consequences will weigh on the calculations of any leader who contemplates nuclear war. All
war involves risk. Nuclear war carries with it risks that
no leader of the past ever had to face, and that no leader
of the future is likely to wish to run.

Nations went to war in the past because they believed
that they could win. A large-scale nuclear war would so
damage the two sides engaged in it as to call into question
the very idea of victory. This is a revolutionary feature

of nuclear weapons for which there is no precedent. It is in this sense that these weapons are different from any that have ever existed before. The destruction from a nuclear exchange would be so great that it is questionable whether the conflict would deserve to be described as a war. War implies the use of force for some political purpose. It is difficult to imagine a political purpose that would be served by the slaughter and devastation that even a handful of nuclear weapons would bring to the societies at which they were aimed.

The nuclear future, at least to the year 2000, is likely to follow a middle path between disarmament and nuclear war. Nuclear weapons will continue to exist but will not be used, at least not by the United States and the Soviet Union against each other on a large scale. This is the most important thing to say about the nuclear future. But it is not the only thing to say.

What remains to be said is contained in the answers to two questions. The first is: Given that there will continue to be nuclear weapons, how many of what types will there be, who will own them, and how and where will they be deployed? The second question is: Short of the most dramatic and sweeping effect—nuclear war— what influence will these weapons have on international politics? That is, what will the world look like and what difference will nuclear weapons make?

The basis for the nuclear deployments of the next two decades will be the weapons that exist now. What the world will look like in the year 2000 will be some modified version of what it looks like now. Similarly, the political influence of nuclear weapons in the future will have something to do with the influence they have already had.

What the world looks like now is easy to describe.

[25]

There are a great many nuclear weapons—estimates range up to fifty thousand—and most of them are in the control of the United States and the Soviet Union. Both have been designated "nuclear superpowers," to signify that their nuclear firepower not only lifts them above other countries in the contemporary international system but also gives them much more destructive force than the great powers of the past had.

The first two bombs drew their explosive power from fission—the process of splitting apart the heart of the atom. Their destructive power was measured in equivalence to thousands of tons of TNT. The weapons possessed by both the United States and the Soviet Union today draw their destructive force from nuclear fusion, the process of fusing atoms together. Fusion generates more power than fission. The power of some fusion or hydrogen bombs is measured in equivalence to millions of tons of TNT. Each side has thousands of hydrogen bombs, bombs hundreds and even thousands of times more powerful than the two that crushed Hiroshima and Nagasaki. "There is an immense gulf between the atomic and the hydrogen bomb," Winston Churchill observed. "The atomic bomb, with all its terror, did not carry us outside the scope of human control or manageable events in thought or action, in peace or war. But . . . [with] the hydrogen bomb the entire foundation of human affairs was revolutionized."

Hydrogen bombs are not a thousand times as destructive as atomic bombs. Destructiveness increases by a fraction of the "yield" of a bomb—its TNT equivalence. When the yield of one bomb is a thousand times that of another, the ratio of destructiveness between the first and the second is less than 1,000 to 1. One implication of this

[26]

fact is that increasing the number of separate bombs expands total destruction faster than increasing the yield of particular ones. For both superpowers, bombs have proved easy and relatively cheap to produce. Moreover, yield measures only one of the lethal effects of nuclear weapons, their blast. There are two others: intense heat—much of Hiroshima was consumed by fire after the bomb struck—and poisonous radioactivity, which lingers long after the bomb has exploded.

Nuclear weapons are often classified according to where they are located and where they are aimed. This classification system has three categories. *Strategic* weapons are placed within the borders of the Soviet Union and the United States or on oceangoing submarines, and are aimed at the homeland of the other superpower. *Intermediate-range* weapons are based in Western Europe and targeted against the Soviet Union, and in the Soviet Union aimed at Western Europe. *Tactical* nuclear weapons are located in Western Europe and designed to strike Eastern Europe, not the Soviet Union, and vice versa. Western tactical nuclear weapons may also be used against invading Warsaw Pact forces that have already reached Western territory. This classification system is used in superpower negotiations. It is arbitrary. It does not include all the nuclear weapons the two great powers have—the United States can fire them from carrier-based aircraft, for example. Moreover, the United States and the Soviet Union have not always agreed, in trying to negotiate limits on their arsenals, on which weapons belong in which categories.

Nuclear weapons are also classified according to the "delivery vehicles" that carry them to their targets. Both sides have weapons that can be fired from land, sea, and air. Both strategic arsenals include ballistic missiles that are based in reinforced concrete silos in the middle of both countries and are capable of striking the other within half an hour of being launched. They include as well oceangoing submarines carrying missiles similar to those based on land but capable of beginning their journeys of destruction from beneath the surface of the sea. And they include manned bomber aircraft able to fly over oceans and continents and drop nuclear explosives in the form of the gravity bombs that are the staple of air warfare or missiles that can propel themselves after airborne launch. The United States also has planes based on aircraft carriers capable of launching nuclear strikes against the Soviet Union. Each superpower has nuclear-tipped missiles and nuclear-weapon-carrying aircraft of intermediate and tactical range as well.

Both the United States and the Soviet Union, therefore, can launch large-scale nuclear attacks from land, sea, and air from every corner of the planet. There is no precedent for this kind of firepower.

The basis of the nuclear-weapons policy of the United States and—although this can be said with less confidence—of the Soviet Union is deterrence. Deterrence is the central concept of the nuclear age. Those who have thought about the political implications of the nuclear revolution have invested considerable time and energy in refining this concept. Deterrence is what has made possible the middle way between the dream of disarmament and the nightmare of nuclear war.

Deterrence means prevention by threat. One party tries to keep another from doing something by threatening some sort of punishment in retaliation. The idea is scarcely a new one. It is probably as old as conflict between sovereign political communities. An ancient Roman saying summarizes it: "Si vis pacem bellum para"—if you want peace, prepare for war.

Deterrence is defensive in intent. The success of a deterrence policy depends on whether the threat is credible—that is, whether it will be carried out—and how serious the injury will be if it is carried out.

Nuclear weapons lend themselves particularly well to deterrence. No other purpose besides defense—indeed, almost no other purpose besides the prevention of their own use—has thus far seemed plausible for them. The bombings of Hiroshima and Nagasaki were, it is true, undertaken for a different purpose. Japan did surrender after they took place. But in the history of the nuclear era these cases now seem exceptional. A country that tried to conquer another with a nuclear attack would render worthless the territory it hoped to occupy. Of course nuclear weapons are not worthless for offensive purposes. A nuclear-armed country could defeat one without nuclear weapons by using them.

Nuclear weapons lend themselves readily to deterrence, however, because whatever the likelihood that a country will carry out a threat to use them—and the problem of reinforcing credibility has preoccupied the nuclear priesthood—the damage if such a threat *is* carried out would be so grave that it is bound to have some influence. Nuclear weapons will have some deterrent value even if no such a threat is ever explicitly made.

Another, related concept plays an important role in nuclear deterrence: assured destruction. The term was coined by the American branch of the nuclear fraternity. It comes from the realization that nuclear weapons are so powerful that they might be used by one country to strike a disarming blow against the nuclear arsenal of the other. If one side used its nuclear weapons to destroy the nuclear weapons of the other, it would have the other at its mercy. To avoid this outcome, to deter such an attack, a nuclear arsenal would have to be designed so that it could not be completely smashed by a preemptive attack. For one nuclear power facing another, deterrence depends on the assurance of being able to weather an attack with enough firepower to deliver a devastating retaliatory blow against the attacker. The capacity for an assured *second* strike will deter a *first* strike.

"Assured destruction" has been used to refer specifically to the amount of damage the Kennedy administration decided the United States had to be sure of being able to inflict on the Soviet Union in response to the most powerful Soviet assault imaginable in order to be certain of deterring such an assault. The standard has been variously defined as one-fifth to one-third of the Soviet population and one-half to three-quarters of Soviet industrial capacity.

The definition is largely arbitrary. It was based on only the most speculative reading of the psychology of the Soviet leadership. It seems plausible that the promise of considerably less destruction would discourage any sane leader from attacking the United States. When the standard was set, the United States already had enough firepower to inflict the designated levels of destruction. The definition was proposed partly to set a limit on the American stockpile of nuclear weapons, a limit beyond which more weapons would be unnecessary, a limit that both the United States and the Soviet Union have now considerably exceeded.

The concept of assured destruction has another significance. It serves as a guideline for deciding which nuclear weapons to produce. It implies that the weapons
that are desirable are the ones that can survive an initial, disarming assault and be used for a second strike.
The concept of assured destruction is the reason that
land-based missiles of both sides have been placed in
hardened underground silos. It is the reason President
Kennedy ordered that a certain number of B-52 bomber
aircraft be airborne at all times and thus immune to destruction on the ground. The ideal instrument of assured
destruction, and therefore the ideal weapon for deterrence, is the submarine. Its ability to move about in the
vast depths of the world's oceans makes it safe from
surprise attack. It is axiomatic that, absent the kind of
breakthrough in the techniques of antisubmarine warfare that cannot now be foreseen, submarines on station
would survive any assault, whatever happened to the
other nuclear-weapon delivery vehicles, and be ready to
fire their missiles in a retaliatory strike.

Both the United States and the Soviet Union have
enough survivable firepower to devastate the other even
after absorbing a massive blow. The capacity for assured
destruction is mutual. The two superpowers' relationship
of mutual assured destruction is sometimes abbreviated
by the acronym MAD. It is an acronym that expresses
a widely felt unease about the security of the world's
basic nuclear arrangements. The policy of deterrence
through the capacity for assured destruction is a policy
of self-defense by means of a threat to incinerate millions of people in response to an attack. It is not a threat
that any sane leader would feel comfortable in carrying
out, and it has been criticized on this ground.

[31]

The *capacity* for assured destruction, however, is the result not of the particulars of American or Soviet deterrence policy but of the physical properties of nuclear weapons themselves. The decision to have nuclear armaments is a decision to be able to crush other countries. As long as nuclear weapons exist, they will threaten mass destruction, which in turn will influence other countries, whether or not the governments of the countries that have the weapons make that threat publicly and explicitly.

Only the United States and the Soviet Union have nuclear arsenals with the unchallengeable capacity for the assured destruction of the other. Three other countries, however, have nuclear weapons. Britain, France, and China have far less nuclear firepower than the two superpowers, and less influence in international affairs. Their weapons are not, however, without significance. While they are dwarfed by what the superpowers have, they still far surpass in destructive power anything available before 1945. In relative terms—and it is relative measures of power that count in international politics—all three countries have been much less important in the second half of the twentieth century than in previous eras. But by absolute standards the present leader of each controls far more destructive force than was dreamed of by Lord Palmerston or Louis XIV or the Kiang-hsi emperor, each of whom played a far greater role in world affairs than his contemporary successor could hope to do.

British scientists took part in the Manhattan Project, and Britain exploded its first bomb in 1952. Now there are 64 British submarine-based missiles, which are due to be replaced with more capable ones in the late 1980s, and 60 bombers capable of hitting targets in the Soviet Union. The British nuclear arsenal is formally part of the nuclear forces of the North Atlantic Treaty Organization, all the rest of which are controlled by the United States. Britain would conduct a nuclear war independently of NATO only in the event of a "national emergency," the nature of which the British government has never publicly defined.

France, which became a nuclear power in 1960, formally dissociated itself from the NATO military command in 1965. France's 80 submarine-launched ballistic missiles and 40 medium-range bombers are officially available only for the defense of France. Both its withdrawal from NATO and its nuclear weapons program were part of a policy of trying to assert an independent French role in world affairs. France is, however, closely aligned with the United States and the rest of Western Europe, and a French nuclear salvo independent of any NATO engagement is unlikely. The likeliest occasion for the use of the French nuclear arsenal would be a Soviet attack on France. France is separated from Soviet forces in Europe, however, by West Germany, a central member of NATO. It is difficult, therefore, to imagine France engaged in a war in which NATO, and thus the United States, would not be involved.

Unlike Britain and France, the People's Republic of China is not allied to or unambiguously aligned with the United States. China does not, it is true, stand equidistant between the two great nuclear powers. Since the early 1970s it has been closer to the United States. There is no defense treaty between the two, however, nor is China located in the middle of a region the United States has pledged to defend, as France is.

China's approximately 100 medium-range ballistic missiles and its like number of medium-range aircraft, all capable of striking the Soviet Union although not the

United States, are more likely to be used against the Soviets independently of the Americans than is the French nuclear arsenal. They may have come close to being used. In 1969 fighting broke out along the border between China and the Soviet Union. It is the only direct military engagement between two countries with nuclear weapons in history, but neither used its nuclear armaments.

Although China is more independent of the United States in nuclear terms than Britain and France, like the other two China is far inferior to the two superpowers in nuclear might. Like them it does not have substantial influence beyond its own borders. Like them it has not taken on the task of protecting other countries with its nuclear arsenal. So although there are at least three independent nuclear arsenals, three independent centers of nuclear decision, the world is very far from having three major nuclear powers. The international system is, to use the terms common within the cadre of nuclear experts, bipolar, not tripolar.

The existence of these weapons may have had the profoundest possible effect on international politics. They may have prevented a third world war. Without nuclear weapons the world would still have been divided, as it has been, into two camps, headed by the United States and the Soviet Union. The American coalition would have included, as it does now, North America, Western Europe, Japan, and conceivably, at some point, China. The Soviet Union would have held sway over Eastern Europe.

In the postwar period not only has there been no war between these two camps, but the Western coalition has never gone very far in mobilizing its resources for military purposes. The Western Europeans and especially the

Japanese devote only a small fraction of their national wealth to defense. This restraint, it may be argued, can be attributed to their confidence that the American nuclear arsenal will prevent a Soviet attack. Since war is not likely, there is no point in making extensive preparations to fight. To put it differently, nuclear weapons have meant that the Western coalition has felt confident of being able to deter the Soviet Union with relatively little effort.

Without nuclear weapons the members of the Western coalition would not have wished to go to war, but might well have been drawn into one. Since 1945 the Soviet Union has felt threatened and has behaved aggressively. The Soviets' forcible imposition of Communist governments in Eastern Europe, their maintenance of a huge standing army on both eastern and western borders, and their occupation of the southern islands of the Kurile chain, which have traditionally belonged to Japan, have done a great deal to create the coalition that opposes them. There is a striking parallel between the years since World War II and the period leading up to World War I. Soviet foreign policy has been largely the product of ambitions and anxieties that are similar to those that animated imperial Germany between 1900 and 1914. It has been marked by the same combination of bellicosity and clumsiness. Before 1914 there were no nuclear weapons to impose caution.

This comparison may be carried one step further. In World War I, Britain, France, Russia, and ultimately the United States defeated Germany. In resources, and therefore in military potential, the Soviet Union is at an even greater disadvantage than Germany was in the face of an opposing coalition. The probable outcome of a war fought without nuclear weapons after 1945, and certainly after the economic recovery of Japan and Western Europe in the 1950s, was a defeat for the Eastern bloc. It therefore may be that the Soviet Union owes its existence, at least in its present form as a latter-day successor to the multinational empires of Central and Eastern Europe, to nuclear weapons.

It may equally be argued, however, that nuclear weapons have made no appreciable difference at all in international politics; or, at most, have reinforced a trend that would have been powerful without them. The United States and the Soviet Union would have emerged from World War II as the international system's two strongest powers even in a nonnuclear world. They would undoubtedly have been rivals whatever their weaponry. But each might well have been eager to avoid fighting the other. Both had gained territory and influence as a result of the war, although at a terrible price, especially in the Soviet case. Neither had claims on lost territory. World War II had been bloody and destructive, and its example alone might have served to discourage another great conflict.

The advent of nuclear weapons has overshadowed that example, and it has overshadowed as well the advances in nonnuclear weaponry that have taken place since 1945. But as a result of these developments, World War III would be much more destructive than World War II even if it were not fought with nuclear weapons.

Whatever the influence of nuclear weapons, the two nuclear superpowers have avoided war with each other. They have not avoided fighting other, nonnuclear countries, however. The United States has waged two substantial wars in Asia, on the Korean peninsula and in the former French possessions of Indochina. The Soviet Union has sent troops into Hungary, Czechoslovakia, and Afghanistan. In none of these instances were nuclear weapons used.

The reasons for this restraint are not easy to fix with precision. Nuclear weapons were, or at least seemed to be, inappropriate for many of the military tasks the superpowers undertook. Each was no doubt worried about nuclear retaliation by the other even when the other's forces were not directly engaged. Moral scruples about subjecting more people to what those in Hiroshima and Nagasaki experienced in August 1945 have certainly not been negligible.

Although nuclear weapons have not been used since 1945, moreover, the veiled suggestion by the United States that they might be used seems to have had some influence—in ending the Korean war, for instance, and in discouraging military operations in the Taiwan Straits by the People's Republic of China in the 1950s. The argument that nuclear armaments have had a pacifying effect in East Asia, as in Europe, is plausible, if not susceptible to proof.

Although the effects of the existence of nuclear weapons in the past are difficult to judge, the question of how changes in the number, types, and distribution of nuclear weapons will influence international politics over the next two decades is not entirely unmanageable. Those changes are likely to be marginal. The world will look roughly as it does today. There will be many nuclear weapons, in more or less the same hands.

What changes are likely? Whatever they are, they will be the products of three things. One is the improvement of the technology of nuclear weaponry, which takes the form of the arms race between the United States and the Soviet Union. The second is the spread of nuclear weapons to countries that do not have them. The term that the nuclear priesthood has coined for this process and that has come into common use is "proliferation." The third force bearing on the nuclear future has already made the early years of the 1980s distinctive by making that future a prominent topic of the ongoing public conversation in the West. The third force is public opinion, and especially those segments of it represented by the anti–nuclear weapons movements in the United States and Europe.

[2]

The Arms Race

The most basic reason that there has been, and will continue to be, a nuclear arms race between the United States and the Soviet Union is the same reason that they, and other countries, have weapons in the first place: the anarchy of international politics creates insecurity, which makes self-protection prudent and weapons necessary.

In the nuclear age the United States and the Soviet Union not only have had weapons, they have competed to build more and better ones. Their ongoing competition has its roots in a modern development—indeed, the development that some would say is the most important of the modern era: the Industrial Revolution. The Industrial Revolution, which began in the last quarter of the eighteenth century in England and continues today almost everywhere, has substituted machines for human and animal power to carry out social tasks. One of those is warfare.

The Industrial Revolution has furnished progressively more powerful and more efficient machinery. Since the end of the eighteenth century the world has seen a steady stream of new inventions, for agriculture, transportation, communication, and other human endeavors, including fighting. It has been said that the Industrial Revolution's most important invention was the *idea* of invention.

Once that idea took root, it created an expectation of regular improvement in machines of various sorts. Commercial firms required the latest machines to be profitable. Otherwise their competitors would make better, cheaper goods and take away their markets. Similarly, countries in the industrial age have needed the latest machines of war to remain secure. If they did not get them, they have feared, others would, with potentially disastrous consequences. Nuclear weapons are no less the products of the Industrial Revolution than indoor plumbing, automobiles, refrigerators, and the equipment in modern hospitals. As with other industrial products, the United States and the Soviet Union have competed strenuously to have more and better models.

The development of nuclear weapons by scientists recalls the story of Dr. Frankenstein, whose genius created a rampaging monster. Like him, the atomic scientists have had qualms about their handiwork. They have in fact been at the forefront of efforts to restrain the arms race. The chief obstacle to stopping it is that there are *two* groups of scientists and *two* sets of laboratories, two monsters in the form of large nuclear arsenals. Neither side has felt able to let the other make larger, fiercer, more deadly monsters while it did nothing.

There is another reason for the steady growth of the world's two main arsenals. Adding to them serves the interests of particular groups in both the United States and the Soviet Union. The American armed forces want the most sophisticated missiles, ships, and aircraft that can be built. Contracts to build them are the lifeblood of defense industries, and they often lobby the Congress to authorize funds for weapons projects in which they hope to participate. The various groups that tend to favor large defense budgets, including funds for the acquisition of more nuclear weapons, are sometimes lumped together under the heading "the military-industrial complex," a term that Dwight Eisenhower introduced in his final public speech as president, when he warned against the undue influence of these groups.

The Soviet economic and political systems differ radically from the American models. There is some evidence, nonetheless, that a military-industrial complex exists in the Soviet Union, too. The ministries with jurisdiction over large, complicated, expensive weapons, and especially nuclear weapons, are thought to press the central leadership to assign resources to build them. Larger orders do not bring profit to the relevant departments, but rather power and prestige within the Soviet government.

The role of the military-industrial complex in shaping each country's nuclear arsenal may be significant but it is secondary. The United States and the Soviet Union have nuclear weapons because the world in which they exist is anarchic. They compete to equip themselves with more and better weapons because technical advance is a normal feature of modern life. The precise numbers and types of nuclear armaments each has come to have are the result of the interplay of political forces in which domestic groups, with their own particular reasons for wanting to expand their country's nuclear arsenal, have had important roles. Since neither side is going to drop out of the arms race, and since the conditions responsible for it will persist in the absence of some overarching political agreement to stop it that is not now in sight, the Soviet-American arms race will continue into the twenty-first century.

Although nuclear weapons, like other industrial products, have improved continually, some improvements in the techniques of mass destruction have been more important than others. The most important innovations of all were the first controlled nuclear fission and the initial two bombs, which proved that the energy at the heart of matter predicted by Einstein's theory and demonstrated by the discovery of radioactivity, could be harnessed. The next major innovation, both chronologically and in importance, was the fusion bomb, which was unambiguously a weapon of mass destruction. The third major innovation in nuclear weaponry was the capacity for making bombs cheaply. These events followed a familiar industrial sequence. The prototypes required a great deal of time and effort to make; the Manhattan Project was a costly venture that lasted several years. Ultimately, however, the manufacture of nuclear explosives became routine. Not only did the United States and the Soviet Union have access to the energy at the heart of matter, not only could they make explosives based on fusion as well as fission, but they could make them on a large scale. Each has been able to afford thousands. For the United States, especially, nuclear weapons have been relatively inexpensive. In the 1970s nuclear expenses consumed less than 10 percent of the overall defense budget. The final landmark innovation was the ballistic missile. It represented an advance not in the design of nuclear explosives themselves but in the capacity to deliver them to distant targets. Missiles are more expensive than bombs. But both superpowers have several thousand, of various ranges. Both can therefore hurl bombs thousands of miles in a matter of a few minutes.

Each of these major innovations in nuclear weaponry came relatively early in the nuclear age. The last of them, the ballistic missile, dates from the late 1950s. So to the extent that the world's present nuclear arrangements are based on these technical developments, they were in place, or at least their outline was clear, more than two decades ago. These arrangements, whose centerpiece is the relationship of mutual assured destruction between the United States and the Soviet Union, were made inevitable by another feature that the major nuclear innovations have in common: all of the innovations favor the offense. All have made the task of destruction easier, that of preventing destruction harder and more costly. The technical developments in nuclear weaponry since 1960 have, with a few exceptions, had the same effect.

The great missing innovation in the nuclear age is the development of the means to defend against nuclear attack. If it were available it would have far-reaching consequences. It would be as momentous as any of the landmark innovations of the past. It would in fact be as momentous as all of them put together, since it would negate their combined effect. If the defense against nuclear weapons dominated their offensive power, the world would be a more comfortable place to live in. Deterrence through mutual assured *protection* is a more agreeable prospect than deterrence by mutual assured destruction.

Mounting an effective defense against nuclear attack is a formidable task. Indeed, it is probably impossible. A system of defense would have to be perfect. The first and second major innovations in nuclear weaponry have made each individual bomb extraordinarily powerful. If a city were attacked by 100 explosives and 99 were turned away, the city would still be destroyed. And perfect defense is probably unattainable because of the third and fourth major nuclear innovations. Each side can hurl 100 bombs at many of the other's cities, from all over the world at an almost infinite variety of speeds and altitudes, in different flight patterns, along with many decoys and devices designed to defeat defenses, and still have a plentiful supply of nuclear firepower left.

No machine, let alone the complicated combination of machines that would make up a system of defense against ballistic missiles, ever works without a hitch, especially when it is first used. None of the antiaircraft batteries of World War II ever prevented all bombs from falling on the cities they were defending during large air raids. But ballistic missile defense would have to work perfectly from the start.

The idea of defense against nuclear attack, like the idea of disarmament, is an appealing and therefore a recurrent one. It has often been coupled with proposals for programs of civil defense. But even when the two are combined, complete protection from catastrophic destruction seems a fantasy. The underground shelters on which suggested civil defense programs often rely are designed to protect civilians only from the fallout from nuclear explosions, not from the blast or heat. Fallout shelters might save lives in a nuclear war, but only shelters at considerable distances from the landing sites of bombs. Other programs call for the evacuation of civilians from areas where bombs are likely to fall. This strategy presumes that the other side will be good enough to spare the places to which people are evacuated, and that the currents of radioactive air created by the blasts will go elsewhere.

Defense against nuclear attack is either perfect or worthless. The United States and the Soviet Union have decided that it cannot be perfected. This assumption is enshrined in the 1972 ABM Treaty, which forbids each signatory to build ballistic missile defenses for more than two cities. (The permitted number was later reduced to one. The United States has none.) Both countries agreed to the treaty because the task of building a perfect defense system seemed beyond their powers. They wanted to prevent a costly competition in defense systems that would not, in the end, protect either society from the bombs of the other. Despite the treaty, both sides continue research on ballistic missile defense, as a hedge against a technical breakthrough by the other.

New technologies are in fact looming on the horizon which promise better systems than could be constructed in the past. The highly concentrated beams of light known as lasers and equally powerful particle beams hold out hope for effective defense. This is, at best, a distant hope. Whatever the ultimate prospects for them, they will not make possible working, foolproof protective machinery before the year 2000. It may be an entirely vain hope. "What matters," according to the British scientist Lord Zuckerman, "is whether an ABM system could be devised which would give a country's political leader the assurance that nuclear fire from the enemy would not be able to destroy his vital cities. . . . In my view the answer will always be NO, for the good and simple reason that in any theoretical nuclear scenario it will always be possible to saturate an ABM system with an avalanche of missiles, not to mention strike those targets which may not be protected."

The history of warfare, especially the branch of it that concerns the evolution of weaponry, is the history of an ongoing contest between offense and defense. The weapons at hand have sometimes conferred advantage on the would-be conqueror, sometimes on the side resisting at-

[45]

tack. The Industrial Revolution intensified the contest because it produced a steady flow of innovations relevant to both attack and defense and because it spread the contest from the land and sea to the air. It is a revolutionary feature of nuclear weapons that they appear to have brought the contest to an end by giving a decisive and irrevocable advantage to the offense. The appearance, however, is partly deceptive; matters are a bit more complicated.

There are three ways for a country to defend itself. The most obvious is protection, warding off an attack to prevent the enemy army from seizing territory. Historically protection has been the normal method of defense. That is what defense ordinarily means. Defense is also possible through deterrence, keeping others at bay by threatening punishment in response to an attack. For most of recorded history, deterrence was a by-product of the capacity for protection. A country that did not believe that it could defeat another was unlikely to try, and was therefore deterred from making war.

In the nuclear age, however—and this is another revolutionary difference between nuclear armaments and all others—protection and deterrence have become quite distinct for the United States and the Soviet Union. Each could punish the other with an annihilating assault in response to an attack against which neither could protect itself. The certainty that each side could, if it chose, inflict enormous destruction in retaliation for an initial attack deters each side from launching such an attack, even though the other side could not protect itself. Indeed, retaliation is certain *because* protection is impossible. Mutual assured destruction is a relationship of defense for both sides through the superiority of the offense of each.

The third way a country might defend itself is by pre-emption, by knocking out the forces of an adversary in a preemptive attack. Preemption differs from prevention in its timing, in that it requires the putative defender to strike first, and in the point of contact between the two forces, which is located within the territory of the putative attacker, not that of the preempting defender.

Defense by preemption is as difficult in the nuclear era as defense by protection. It, too, would have to be perfect to ensure victory. Thousands of weapons would have to be destroyed more or less simultaneously so that none could be fired in a retaliatory assault. The delivery vehicles carrying nuclear explosives that would have to be destroyed in a preemptive attack are fewer and larger, and therefore better targets, than the explosives themselves, which would be the objects of defense by prevention. The task of protection, on the other hand, is confined to the territory of the country attempting to defend itself, whereas the theater of operations for preemption is the entire planet.

Moreover, one particular kind of delivery vehicle is presently immune to preemptive attack. Missile-bearing submarines are triply safe: they can lurk in almost any part of the planet covered by the oceans; underwater they are hard to find; and they can move. The agent of preemption that has received most attention within as well as outside the circle of nuclear specialists is the accurate land-based missile, which can strike targets in other countries with growing precision. For the future of deterrence the techniques of antisubmarine warfare, usually abbreviated as ASW, are more significant. Only if the techniques for tracking and destroying submarines at sea improve more dramatically than is now anticipated would the relationship of mutual assured destruction be

[47]

at risk. Such improvements, if they are ever possible, will not occur before the year 2000. Neither the United States nor the Soviet Union, therefore, will be able to disarm the other. Neither will have what is called a first-strike capacity.

Although neither protection nor preemption is now feasible, in the arms competition between the United States and the Soviet Union the two means of defense have received different treatment. While the impossibility of mounting a perfect defense by protection against nuclear attack has caused the two sides to promise, through the ABM Treaty, not even to try to do so, the comparable difficulties of total defense by preemption have not kept either from acquiring the *partial* capacity for defense of this sort. The reason is that defense by preemption is a by-product of the improvements in *offensive* weaponry that the two sides have regularly made.

Recent technical advances have made limited, though not total, defense by preemption seem increasingly possible. The guidance systems with which missiles are equipped have been improved. Each side is better able to track, aim at, hit, and destroy the missiles (as well as the airplanes on the ground and the submarines in port) of the other side than ever before. So the arms race has become in part a version of the age-old contest. On one side are forces capable of defense by preemption, including more powerful warheads that can destroy the other side's armaments, more sophisticated surveillance equipment to track those armaments, and especially more accurate guidance systems to direct the bombs and warheads to the targets that the surveillance equipment has pinpointed. On the other side are measures to protect weapons against preemptive attack, by reinforcing the shelters in which they are based, moving them around, even concealing them. It is a contest between destruction and evasion, between hitting and dodging.

Weapons suitable for preemption pose a particular problem for the Soviet-American nuclear relationship. Preemptive military operations, even if designed for defensive purposes, are precisely those an aggressor would launch. Preemption has ordinarily been the strategy of the conqueror, not the defender. And if a first strike is successful, the attacker has the defender at its mercy and can reap the benefits of conquest even if those benefits were not originally sought.

Preemptive weapons—that is, weapons suitable for mounting a first strike—are usually presumed to signal aggressive intentions. Such weapons are therefore inconsistent with deterrence through mutual assured destruction, which assumes that each side aims at the cities and industry of the other side, not at its weapons. Assured destruction means destruction of civilian, not military targets. Aiming at civilians is assumed to show defensive, benign intentions because it would be sensible to launch such an attack, if at all, only in retaliation for a previous attack. Hitting cities would be sensible, that is, only in a *second* strike. To aim at weapons suggests an interest in launching a disarming strike. It therefore suggests a willingness to start a war. If each side aims at cities, neither displays any interest in beginning hostilities. Both signal plans to strike *second*, not first. If nobody strikes first, there is no war. The result is stability—that is, a stable balance of power, or terror. The capacity to destroy weapons is therefore destabilizing. This is the origin of the maxim that expresses the grim paradoxical logic of deterrence through mutual assured destruction: "Killing weapons is bad. Killing people is good." Or, to put it in more technical terms, weapons suitable for "counter-value" attacks are preferable to those for "counterforce."

The problem could be avoided if the two sides refrained from developing armaments suitable for counterforce attacks. This strategy would require both sides to keep the yields of warheads small. They would also have to limit the numbers of warheads—it is possible to mount several on each missile—so as to keep the ratio of bombs to targets low enough to prevent each side from being confident of knocking out the other's missiles. They would have to shun the computers and inertial guidance systems that have made missiles so accurate. Neither side, however, has been willing, or able, to practice the necessary self-restraint.

Despite these technical developments, it is worth emphasizing, neither the United States nor the Soviet Union has any foreseeable prospect of having a first-strike capacity. Neither has any hope of rendering the other wholly impotent in nuclear terms with a disarming blow. No matter how many of the other's weapons each will have the means to cripple, both will have enough nuclear firepower in reserve—if only on submarines—to turn the other's cities to rubble and ashes.

If they will be equal in the capacity for assured destruction in the year 2000, however, the United States and the Soviet Union will not be equal in all the details of their nuclear arsenals, including the capacity for counterforce attacks. To the contest between preemption and preservation the two sides bring different assets. The Americans have technical advantages. They are better able to design and build sophisticated armaments. But in the United States public opposition can block the deployment of weapons that the government favors. At different times various segments of the public in the United States and in other NATO countries as well have made it clear that they do not want the enhanced radiation warhead (commonly called the neutron bomb), the MX missile, and the extended-range Pershing missiles and ground-launched cruise missiles scheduled for deployment in Western Europe to be placed near them, or in some cases to be placed anywhere.

The two arsenals differ now in other ways. Soviet land-based missiles are larger than American ones, but more vulnerable to preemptive attack. The total yield of the Soviet missile force is larger, but the American force, counting submarines and bombers, has more warheads. The contrast is between brute strength and agility. The Soviet Union has a smaller fleet of intercontinental bombers than does the United States. It is debatable whether the most capable Soviet long-range bomber, the Backfire, truly qualifies as a strategic weapon comparable to the American B-52. The Soviet Union, however, has built thick networks of defense against bombers (though not, of course, against ballistic missiles) while the United States has not. The United States, in turn, has more capable submarines. They have greater ranges, can operate more quietly and are thus freer from detection, and have more advantageous bases than their Soviet counterparts.

These differences are of long standing, and are unlikely to disappear between the present and the year 2000. So to the first question, What will the two nuclear arsenals look like?, the answer is that they are likely to be larger, more versatile, and more capable than they are now, but not identical. The actual and expected differences between them, especially in the capacity for counterforce attacks, has been the focus of a continuing debate within the American nuclear fraternity, which is in fact a debate about the second question that is relevant for the nuclear future: What differences will these dissimilarities make?

One school of thought denies that foreseeable asymmetries will have any significant consequences, military or political. The reason for this view is the special property of nuclear weapons, their extraordinary destructive power, which gives both sides the capacity for assured destruction.

The argument may be illustrated by analogy to the relationship between gold and paper money under a pure gold standard. Paper currency has no value in itself. It could serve as a medium of exchange when all buyers and sellers understood that it could be redeemed for the amount of gold equivalent in value to its denomination. As long as everybody was certain that the exchange could be made, it did not have to be made. Paper was as good as gold. In fact, when paper became credible as a medium of exchange, it was superior to gold, because it was easier to use. It is awkward to carry around a supply of gold for ordinary transactions.

Under most circumstances military might and political influence stand in something like the same relationship to each other as gold and paper. A powerful country can have its way in a political conflict with a lesser one without fighting when both understand that if they were to fight, the powerful one would win. Because weapons can be "cashed in"—that is, used to achieve military victory and thus political goals—and both sides recognize this fact, the weapons do not have to be used. Fighting wars, like carrying around a supply of gold, is inconvenient at best.

What is different about the relationship between the United States and the Soviet Union is that neither could inflict total defeat by rendering the other helpless no matter how many weapons it had. This is the significance of assured destruction. In an all-out war each could destroy the other no matter what the differences between their nuclear forces. Assured destruction is an absolute, not a relative standard. Neither can deprive the other of it.

A conflict between two countries with the capacity for assured destruction would not be a contest to eliminate the military forces of the other side. By definition neither has this ability. It would be a competition in risk taking. One side would try to make the other back down for fear of having its cities smashed, even though its own cities could be smashed too. What would matter, in the words of political scientist Robert Jervis, would be not the balance of military forces but the balance of *resolve* between the two. The more determined country, the one more willing to run risks, would probably get what it wanted. Determination has nothing necessarily to do with who has what nuclear weapons over and above those required for assured destruction.

The argument has a clear implication for the size of each superpower's nuclear arsenal. If discrepancies beyond the level of assured destruction do not affect international politics, then neither side needs *any* nuclear weapons beyond that level. In that case, both sides have many more armaments than are necessary. Former secretary of defense Robert McNamara once estimated that a nuclear force totaling 400 equivalent megatons—that is, 400 million tons of TNT equivalence—in yield would be enough to inflict unacceptable damage on the Soviet

Union; the Kremlin would not risk incurring this much destruction. The present American nuclear arsenal is close to ten times that powerful, the Soviet arsenal by this measure more powerful still. The weapons both sides have beyond what they need for assured destruction represent, by this logic, at best a waste of money.

A relatively small number of nuclear weapons can give a country the capacity for assured destruction, provided that they are invulnerable to preemptive attack. A few nuclear-armed submarines, conceivably even just one, would be an adequate deterrent force. The idea of placing all the nation's nuclear firepower aboard a single sub-marine has no enthusiasts in the United States. It would be much too risky. But there are those who believe that far fewer nuclear arms than both sides now have would fulfill the purpose that these weapons serve. The posi-tion that they advocate is known as that of "minimum," or "finite," or "pure" deterrence.

Some American nuclear specialists believe that differ-ences do matter even when each side has the unchal-lengeable means to destroy the other in a retaliatory strike. Even if the two arsenals differ only in appearance and not in real military capabilities, they argue, in the world in which the United States and the Soviet Union live, appearances are important. The Soviet-American ri-valry is bound to lead to tests of will, and the side with the larger nuclear arsenal will enjoy a psychological ad-vantage. It will feel more powerful, even if it isn't, and act more aggressively than the other. Appearances are said to be important, as well, because the superpowers compete for the respect and allegiance of other countries, which are apt to be impressed by the larger nuclear stock-pile. The United States, therefore, must be "essentially equivalent" to the Soviet Union in the major categories of nuclear weaponry.

The proponents of assured destruction have replied that the supposed importance of appearances is a flimsy basis for deciding to acquire more and more nuclear armaments. There is no way to know what the most important categories of weaponry are, because there is no way to know what will embolden the Russians or impress other countries. Almost anything might do so. If what counts is what others think about the relationship between the world's two principal nuclear arsenals—if what matter are, to use the term favored in technical discussions, "perceptions"—then the United States is better advised to try to persuade onlookers that such differences as exist have no significance than to attempt to eliminate any and all of them.

The belief that differences between the two arsenals beyond assured destruction are significant rests not mainly on the symbolic import of these differences, however, but rather on their military implications. What counts in this view is not what the two nuclear forces look like, but what they can do.

This argument begins with a particular conception of the nature of the military force that is available to the superpowers. It is to be thought of as falling along a spectrum whose points vary according to how and where battles are fought, and range from the most serious and destructive kind of force—nuclear attacks against American and Soviet cities—to the least serious and destructive (at least from the point of view of the superpowers)—proxy conflicts involving nonnuclear weapons far from Europe or North America. This spectrum is sometimes depicted as a ladder. There are intermediate rungs between the top and the bottom, levels of force less serious than the highest of them, but graver and more dangerous than the lowest.

The argument goes that the United States must match the Soviet Union at each level of force, or at least at each important level. If the United States is inferior at any of them, the Soviet Union can gain an advantage by attacking, or threatening to attack, at that level. The United States would then have to choose between accepting defeat and moving to the next highest rung on the ladder—"escalating" the conflict. There would, however, be strong inhibitions against escalation, for it might get out of control and propel both sides to the very top of the ladder and a mutually disastrous nuclear exchange. The Americans who believe that nuclear imbalances above the level of assured destruction are significant fear that the American president would not risk further escalation and so would accept defeat; or that the Soviet Union would act on the assumption that that is what the American president would do. The Soviets would thus have achieved "escalation dominance." Even if they did not actually attack, they might be able to use the understanding that they could do so and thereby place the United States on the horns of a terrible dilemma. They might behave more aggressively during a confrontation than they would if the two nuclear arsenals were equal in every way.

To avoid conceding escalation dominance to the Soviets, according to this school of thought, the United States needs not just a handful of nuclear weapons that can rain destruction on Russia in response to an attack, but a varied, versatile military force capable of fighting at all the relevant levels of force.

The Arms Race

The term that the Kennedy administration used to describe the military programs that these ideas inspired was "flexible response." The emphasis was on the United States' ability to fight a nonnuclear war in Europe. It was believed that if the Warsaw Pact forces enjoyed preponderance below the nuclear level, they could begin a war and compel the Western coalition to decide between losing and resorting to nuclear weapons. Powerful pressures against making a European war nuclear would inevitably come to bear on NATO. Faced with the choice between "humiliation and holocaust," the West was likely to prefer the first. The Kennedy military program was designed to make it possible to avoid that choice by being able to resist the tanks, planes, and infantry of the Eastern bloc with Western tanks, planes, and infantry—without using nuclear weapons.

The logic of escalation dominance applies, at least in theory, even when nuclear weapons *are* used. If one side launches a "limited" nuclear attack, with tactical, battlefield-range nuclear weapons, or a counterforce salvo with longer-range armaments, the other will arguably be inhibited from escalating for fear of triggering an orgy of city smashing. So if the United States cannot match the Soviet capacity for limited nuclear strikes—that is, for nuclear attacks against targets other than cities—then it may have to choose between losing and risking annihilation.

This logic lies behind the American and Western European worries in the late 1970s and early 1980s about the Soviet SS-20 intermediate-range missile, which is poised to strike targets in Western Europe, and the increasing accuracy of the Soviet fleet of intercontinental ballistic missiles (ICBMS). Each could in theory be used in a counterforce attack, a nuclear strike against military targets that would spare civilians—the SS-20 in Western Europe, the ICBMS in the continental United States. The proponents of the escalation dominance position insisted that the West had to match these armaments. The weapons that were chosen for this purpose, however, proved controversial. The NATO foreign ministers agreed to the deployment of 572 intermediate-range weapons in Europe to offset the SS-20 only on condition that negotiations to reduce or eliminate them take place simultaneously. As for the MX missile, which would give the United States a long-range capacity to strike military targets comparable to that of the Soviet Union, the government had difficulty in finding a politically acceptable way to base it so that it would not be vulnerable to a Soviet preemptive strike even as its technical features were making *Soviet* missiles vulnerable to such an attack.

It has seemed to those who believe in the idea of escalation dominance particularly important that American military forces be capable of fighting at different points along the escalation spectrum. This requirement stems from the country's global responsibilities. The United States is pledged to defend, with nuclear weapons if necessary, nations separated from North America by wide oceans. Thus there are levels of force below nuclear war in North America at which the United States must be able to deter attacks. The capacity for assured destruction alone might suffice to prevent an assault on the United States; but the military forces of the West have to discourage Soviet attacks against Western Europe and Japan as well. The Soviet Union, it has been feared, might not believe that the United States would defend its overseas allies if its only military option were to crush Soviet cities, thereby inviting the incineration of American ones.

The idea of escalation dominance and the prescription for the kinds of military forces the United States requires that follows from it have their critics, particularly those who place their faith in assured destruction. The controversy between the critics and proponents of escalation dominance is in large part a dispute about whether it is in fact possible to fight a "limited" nuclear war. It is a dispute about whether there could be a nuclear engagement that would not leave the two superpowers in ruins.

The critics say that nuclear weapons are so powerful that *any* use of them would cause damage that would not appear "limited" to the country being attacked. Bombs and missiles might go off course in a nuclear war and hit cities even if they were aimed elsewhere. Many civilians could die from strikes that did hit military targets because many such targets in both countries are located in or near populated areas. Skeptics hold, with Lord Zuckerman, that "from the operational point of view there is practically no difference, apart from the verbal one, between what is now called counterforce and what is termed countervalue." If large numbers of its civilians were killed, the country being attacked would have less incentive to avoid striking the attacker's cities.

In any case, the critics note, whatever the damage from the initial nuclear attack, the side that launches it will have to count on restraint by its adversary. It must believe that the other side will not lash out and crush its cities in a retaliatory spasm, something that the other side, if it is the United States or the Soviet Union, would be perfectly capable of doing. How could the attacker be certain that its opponent would not do so?

It could not be certain. No government can ever be certain of another's intentions, or of what the other will eventually do no matter what it originally intends to do. The uncertainty will be especially pronounced when it concerns decisions to be made in the midst, or even in the aftermath, of nuclear explosions. The general point recurs in nuclear affairs. The costs of nuclear war are likely to be so high that when there is a risk of it there will be a powerful tendency for countries to act cautiously. In this case, neither the United States nor the Soviet Union is at all likely to start a limited nuclear war with the other (or perhaps *any* kind of war with the other) because neither could be certain that it would remain limited. And the cost, if it did not, would be too high to risk.

Which view of the political and military uses of nuclear weapons is correct? The idea of escalation dominance requires that nuclear weapons be used with discrimination, that civilians be spared and damage kept limited. Some of the technical developments in weaponry during the 1970s lend themselves to the precision that limited nuclear war requires, notably improved systems of reconnaissance and guidance that have permitted missiles and old-fashioned gravity bombs to be directed to their targets with ever increasing accuracy. The systems have been incorporated in existing weapons, and are likely to be important features of new ones.

The most distinctive new weapon—certainly it is the one whose coming has been most loudly heralded—is likely to be the cruise missile, the small pilotless drone aircraft descended from the "buzz bomb" of World War II, designed to travel at subsonic speed and capable of carrying nuclear or nonnuclear explosives. It assumed a prominent place in American strategic planning during the 1970s because it seemed cheap and unlikely to be covered by the terms of arms-limitation agreements. It has the additional virtue of being suitable for launching from land, sea, and air. All three major branches of the American armed forces—the Army, the Navy, and the Air Force—anticipate deploying cruise missiles.

The role that the cruise missile will play in American— and Soviet—nuclear arsenals between now and the year 2000 is not entirely clear, however. One of its most attractive features becomes dubious upon close scrutiny: its cost. The cost of a cruise missile will depend on the price not only of the missile itself but of the platform from which it is launched. Those platforms may be expensive. The cruise missile's usefulness for the kinds of counterforce missions required by a policy of escalation dominance is also in doubt. Whether cruise missiles can survive preemptive strikes and defeat defenses constructed to thwart them will depend on how many there are, how and where they are deployed, and how much is invested in the task of defending against them, a task that is more feasible than defending against attacks by supersonic ballistic missiles. Even if they survive preemptive strikes and are launched in a retaliatory attack, cruise missiles will fly slowly enough to give the adversary time to fire the weapons at which they are aimed. Cities, unlike weapons, cannot be moved, but hitting cities is not relevant to escalation dominance.

Other, related technical developments may turn out, despite appearances, to be of no use for limited nuclear warfare. There will be improvements in the techniques of battle management. More sophisticated systems of instant communication and information processing as well as guidance will in theory give American and Soviet commanders greater control over their forces in a nuclear battle. They will have a wider choice of targets and more flexibility in timing their attacks. But the facilities for battle management will themselves be vulnerable to attack. They might be quickly destroyed in a nucleár engagement, leaving one or both sides able to conduct only random uncoordinated attacks against the other rather than the measured, careful strikes necessary for escalation dominance.

Still, there is no doubt that both the United States and the Soviet Union will have more accurate weapons in the balance of the twentieth century than they have had before. Each will have some theoretical capacity for nuclear engagements below the level of city destruction. Will either be interested in using that capacity—that is, in fighting, or trying to draw political advantage from threatening to fight, a limited nuclear war?

The history of the nuclear age offers no conclusive evidence on the question. There has been no nuclear war. There has been no direct military conflict of any kind between the United States and the Soviet Union, so the idea of escalation dominance has received no clear test. There have been few direct confrontations between them, tests of will from which the effects of nuclear asymmetries might be inferred. The scarcity of examples on which to base a judgment may itself count against the plausibility of the idea of escalation dominance. It may show that whatever the differences between their nuclear arsenals, the superpowers have invariably dealt with each other cautiously.

There has been one notable confrontation, in the Caribbean in October 1962. The Soviet Union secretly installed in Cuba missiles capable of carrying nuclear weapons to targets in the continental United States. When the American government discovered the missiles, it demanded that they be removed and imposed a naval blockade around the island to demonstrate its seriousness of purpose. For a tense week an armed conflict seemed imminent. Then the Soviets agreed to take the missiles out. The Cuban missile crisis is the closest brush the two nations have had with war with each other. Its outcome lends itself to a variety of interpretations, some of them contradictory. It may be taken to support the idea of escalation dominance: the United States was superior to the Soviet Union and the outcome was an American victory; the Soviet Union was obliged to withdraw the nuclear-capable missiles that it had placed in Cuba.

The outcome of the missile crisis may, however, be irrelevant to the current debate. The idea of escalation dominance holds that differences in nuclear weaponry matter when both sides have the capacity for assured destruction. But in October 1962 the Soviet Union's ability to rain destruction on the United States after absorbing an American attack was by no means assured. Only a few Soviet intercontinental-range missiles were operational at the time. The Soviet bomber fleet was not certain of being able to strike American targets. The Soviet leaders may have decided to put the missiles in Cuba precisely in order to be able to threaten North America.

Alternatively, the outcome of the missile crisis may have been due not to an American advantage in nuclear weaponry but to the overwhelming nonnuclear military superiority of the United States in the Caribbean. If the Soviet Union is regarded as having had the capacity for assured destruction, then this particular interpretation supports the idea of escalation dominance *below* the nuclear threshold. It suggests the need for powerful nonnuclear forces, but implies nothing in particular about nuclear arsenals. If, on the other hand, the Soviet Union did *not* have the capacity to destroy the United States as a functioning society no matter what the Americans did in the fall of 1962, then the outcome of the missile crisis simply demonstrates what has always been true—that military superiority may be translated into political advantage.

It is also possible to see the ending of the crisis as the result of the balance not of military might but of resolve, in which the Americans had the upper hand because geography and history had made the Caribbean more important to the United States than to the Soviet Union. In this view a similar crisis in Eastern Europe probably would have come out differently, with the United States backing down; and it is true that throughout the postwar period, whatever the ratio of forces, nuclear and non-nuclear, the United States has never directly challenged the Soviet Union there.

Finally, it is possible to interpret the outcome of the crisis not as a clear-cut triumph for the United States but as a bargain in which both sides made concessions to avert war. The Soviets did remove their missiles from Cuba. In return the United States pledged not to invade the island and promised to withdraw from Turkey some missiles roughly comparable to those the Soviets had been setting up ninety miles from the Florida coast. This final interpretation lends support to the view that the capacity for assured destruction will deter a wide array of challenges. It suggests that the danger of escalation worried both sides, that each was more interested in finding grounds for accommodation than in scoring political gains at the other's expense, that the specter of catastrophe proved more compelling than the lure of victory.

There is a further difficulty in deciding whether the idea of escalation dominance gives an accurate picture of the relationship between force and politics in the nuclear age. That idea is valid only if the Soviet Union accepts it. For a limited nuclear war to take place, *both* sides must restrain themselves. Soviet views on this issue, as on others, are not wholly clear. Secrecy is the bedrock of the Soviet system.

The Soviets have not entirely succeeded in protecting their nuclear secrets. Nor have Soviet authorities been wholly silent about the purposes their armaments are meant to serve. The difficulty with Soviet nuclear-weapons policy is one of interpretation. It lies not in discovering what Soviet officials have said but in deciding what to make of their statements.

Like the issue of escalation dominance, the question of Soviet attitudes toward nuclear weapons has been the subject of considerable debate in the West. Out of the debate has emerged general, although by no means unanimous, agreement on two points. The first is that Soviet attitudes are not monolithic; there is no single party line on nuclear weapons. Different views are to be found in different parts of the Soviet government. The second is that the dominant Soviet views are different, but not entirely different, from those broadly held in the United States. The Soviets do not contemplate the prospect of nuclear war serenely. They do not appear to be confident that they could win such a war, if winning is taken to mean avoiding terrible damage.

Several distinctions central to American policy, and especially to the idea of assured destruction, do not, however, seem to have the same significance in the Soviet Union. These are the distinctions between counterforce and countervalue weapons, which lend themselves to preemptive strikes in the first case, retaliatory assaults in the second, and therefore imply policies of surprise attack and deterrence respectively. In Soviet thinking counterforce weapons are not necessarily destabilizing. What appears aggressive to Americans is evidently compatible, in Soviet eyes, with defensive intentions. The Soviets apparently regard the visible capacity to fight a nuclear war, to destroy American weapons as well as American cities, as part and parcel of a policy of deterring an American attack. The better they can fight such a war—that is, the more preemptive damage they can do to their adversary's military facilities—they seem to believe, the less likely it is that the West will begin one.

The American and Soviet approaches to nuclear deterrence and warfare have been central to the Western discussion of Soviet nuclear-weapons policy. Those approaches do not, however, bear directly on Soviet attitudes toward escalation dominance. There are reasons to suppose that the idea strikes a responsive chord in the Soviet Union. Soviet literature on international politics stresses that force is to be used for particular political purposes. The Soviet nuclear arsenal is large and varied; it includes weapons of various ranges with ever improving guidance systems.

What the Soviets have said, however, gives the opposite impression. They have consistently denied that gradations of nuclear force have the significance that the idea of escalation dominance imputes to them. They have insisted that once begun, nuclear war cannot and will not remain limited in any meaningful sense of the term. What they have said suggests that they would *not* try hard to reduce casualties in the countries they were attacking. The relevant public statements do not add up to a systematic, authoritative exploration of the issue. They do not prove that escalation dominance is irrelevant to Soviet military planning; at the least, however, they cannot be interpreted as *supporting* the proposition that the idea is central to Soviet nuclear strategy.

Given the weapons that will be available between now and the year 2000—given, that is, what the world will look like—how will this state of affairs affect international politics? Specifically, will superpower relations operate according to the principle of escalation dominance? Is it possible to fight a limited nuclear war? Would a superior capacity to fight one yield political benefits? These questions are central to the nuclear future. No definitive answer to any of them is likely.

Yet it may be predicted that neither side will have sufficient confidence in the idea of escalation dominance to launch an attack. Neither will knowingly provoke another confrontation like the Cuban missile crisis. On the other hand, assured destruction pure and simple is not likely to become the guiding principle for the acquisition and deployment of nuclear weapons by either superpower. Neither side will discard a large fraction of its stockpile. Neither will base its decisions on the number and kinds of weapons to have simply on the belief that the concept of assured destruction or the idea of escalation dominance is correct. Pressure from groups that have particular interests in weaponry—the military-industrial complexes in both countries—will continue to influence decisions on the acquisition of more planes, submarines, and missiles.

And even when doctrine matters, neither side is likely to embrace pure deterrence and rely on a handful of nuclear weapons. It is particularly unlikely that the Soviet

Union will do so. The USSR is a country with a history of insecurity and of arming itself well beyond what seems necessary for territorial defense. The Soviet nuclear arsenal, moreover, is directed not just at the United States but at other members of the Western coalition. Britain, France, and China (a Soviet adversary if not a full-fledged Western ally) have nuclear weapons, and Germany has invaded Russia twice in the twentieth century.

In the United States the idea of pure deterrence has greater appeal. But even the American government will be reluctant to refrain from matching additions to the Soviet nuclear force, no matter how skeptical of the military value of these additions it may be. The political cost of failing to do so if the idea of escalation dominance turns out to be correct will be deemed higher than the purely economic costs of buying excess weapons if it is wrong.

Differences between the two largest nuclear arsenals, then, will probably not provoke attacks, but they will inspire countermeasures. The extreme caution in taking steps with uncertain consequences where nuclear weapons are concerned will push both sides toward restraint in using nuclear weapons but not in having them. The competition in the accumulation of nuclear armaments will continue. It will trouble the public as a whole as well as many nuclear experts. In the future, as in the past, their worries are likely to give rise to efforts to restrain it. As the arms race continues, so will attempts to control it through negotiated agreements.

Negotiations between the United States and the Soviet Union on nuclear weapons have their roots in the impulse for disarmament. The early postwar schemes for the complete abolition, or at least the international control, of nuclear weapons failed, and the search began for some common ground between the superpowers, some measure on which they could agree. It was hoped that agreement would generate trust and goodwill and serve as the "first step" to complete disarmament.

In the 1950s the search for a first step came to center on atomic testing. Although the Soviet and American experimental explosions took place far from populated areas, they produced toxic radioactive fallout that drifted all over the world. In 1963 the two sides concluded a treaty that prohibited testing in the atmosphere, in outer space, and beneath the oceans—but not underground.

The Limited Test Ban Treaty proved a first step not to disarmament but to other modest measures. The Nonproliferation Treaty of 1968, orchestrated by the United States and the Soviet Union, obliged other countries to promise not to get nuclear weapons while the superpowers gave up nothing. In the 1970s the two undertook the Strategic Arms Limitation Talks, or SALT. A freeze on land- and submarine-based ballistic missiles and a treaty effectively prohibiting ballistic missile defense were enacted in 1972. In 1974 the two sides agreed to pursue a new treaty setting equal limits on their offensive strategic weaponry, but it was never submitted by President Gerald Ford to the United States Senate for ratification. In 1979 they finished drafting a treaty that imposed even more comprehensive limits on these weapons. This treaty was submitted for ratification by President Jimmy Carter but then withdrawn after the Soviet invasion of Afghanistan, although the two sides subsequently agreed informally to observe its terms.

The various agreements, ratified and unratified, were modest. Those of 1972, 1974, and 1979 left the United

States and the Soviet Union with more or less the nuclear weapons that they already had, which, by the end of the decade, was a great many indeed in both cases. They imposed limits only on strategic nuclear armaments, not on those of intermediate or tactical range.

They created no international agency to enforce their terms, although a joint Standing Consultative Committee reviews any charges of violation that either brings against the other. As no international body intruded directly on the sovereign prerogatives of either side, a sticking point of the negotiations of the 1950s was avoided. The United States had insisted on being able to monitor any agreement with the Soviet Union, in order to be sure the Soviets were complying with its terms. It insisted that if a test ban were signed, American inspectors must be able to enter the Soviet Union to check on suspicious explosions. The Soviets refused to open their borders to foreign inspectors.

A technical innovation at the beginning of the 1960s broke the impasse and made arms control possible. Reconnaissance satellites went aloft, equipped with powerful cameras that could photograph the military deployments and follow the weapons tests of both countries with great clarity and in fine detail. Each side could thereby count the other's nuclear weapons. No violation of the agreed-upon limits could escape the other's notice. The Soviets could not close their borders to these "eyes in the sky" and did not seriously try to do so.

To win political approval in the United States, a treaty has had to be verifiable. That is, American reconnaissance satellites, and in a few cases electronic monitoring stations, have had to be able to keep track of everything that the Soviet Union has pledged to do and not to do.

The Congress and the American public have had to be convinced that Soviet cheating would not go undetected. The technology of verification grew in sophistication in the 1960s and 1970s. Still, there were limits to each side's powers of detection. Those limits became limits on arms control agreements as well. What could not be verified—and the smaller, more numerous, and easier to hide the weapon, the more difficult it was to monitor—could not be included in a formal agreement.

The cruise missile, which is potentially unverifiable in all of these respects, promises to tax both sides' powers of verification and thus their ability to negotiate meaningful agreements. The need for agreements to be verifiable also produced a conflict between deterrence and arms control. As the accuracies of each side's weapons improved and the other's weapons became vulnerable to preemption, an obvious tactic was to hide them. But hidden weapons are ineligible for inclusion in arms control agreements; what cannot be seen cannot be verified, and what cannot be verified cannot be agreed to. The Carter administration designed an elaborate and expensive system of multiple protective shelters for the MX missile that seemed to have been borrowed from a Rube Goldberg contraption, with tracks for shuttling each missile back and forth among several shelters so that the Soviets would not know where to strike in a preemptive attack. But the shelters also had tops that could be readily opened to permit Soviet satellites to confirm that the United States had fewer missiles than shelters, and had not stored an MX in every one, so that the Soviets could keep an accurate count for the purposes of arms control.

Arms control has not been a purely technical exercise. It has been a deeply, fundamentally political undertaking. Progress has been closely connected to the general state of Soviet-American relations. When the Cold War has been at its coldest, even modest agreements have been impossible to reach. It has been difficult even to carry on negotiations.

The American government has tried on several occasions to alter the relationship. The Nixon administration sought to encourage the Soviets to be better-behaved citizens of the international system by making SALT the centerpiece of a web of ties between the two countries— the others were economic—in which they would become constructively ensnared. They would give up trying to spread their influence by force, it was hoped, for fear of rupturing those ties and risking the benefit of trade. This was the Nixon version of the policy of détente. It did not work. Arms control agreements were modest, economic relations even more so, and Soviet foreign policy showed no sign of being restrained by the fear of losing the chance to have more of either—or at least so a majority of Americans seem to have concluded by the end of the 1970s.

Efforts have also been made to keep arms control and Soviet-American relations in other areas independent of each other. Nuclear negotiations, it has been argued, are too important to be derailed whenever political relations between the superpowers take a turn for the worse. Separation has proved impossible. The hostility between the two nations during most of the 1950s contributed to the fruitlessness of their discussions about arms control then. The Soviet invasion of Czechoslovakia caused the postponement of the opening of the SALT talks in 1968. Soviet activities in southern Africa contributed to the political climate in which President Ford decided not to ask the

Senate to vote on the agreement he had reached on nuclear armaments with his Soviet counterpart, Leonid
Brezhnev, in late 1974. And Jimmy Carter withdrew his
SALT treaty from active consideration in the Senate in 1980
in response to the Soviet invasion of Afghanistan. No
American president has been willing to sit down with the
Soviet leaders or to ask the Senate to ratify a treaty that
he has concluded with them while Soviet troops were
marching into another country, or helping Cubans to
do so.

Arms control has been a contentious political issue in
the United States apart from the vicissitudes of Soviet
foreign policy. Along with the debate between the proponents of escalation dominance and the believers in
assured destruction and the controversy about Soviet
attitudes toward nuclear weapons, the virtues and draw-
backs of arms control as it has been practiced since the
early 1960s has been the third great issue of dispute.
The debate has been partly about the merits of the SALT
II treaty, a complicated document that limited land-based
intercontinental-range ballistic missiles, submarine-
launched missiles, and strategic bombers, and included
special provisions covering missiles with multiple warheads, cruise missiles, the improvements in existing weaponry permitted each side, and the Soviet Backfire bomber,
whose qualifications as a strategic weapon were a subject
of dispute between the two parties. The treaty's critics
charged that it left the Soviet Union with crucial military
advantages, that important parts of its provisions could
not be verified, and that ratifying it would lull Americans
into believing that they were secure and so prevent them
from making the investments in armaments needed to
draw even with the Soviets.

In part the SALT II debate was about the purposes of arms control in general. Even those favorably disposed to the modest agreements that had been achieved over two decades were dismayed that the 1979 treaty had taken so long to negotiate; discussions had begun soon after the 1972 freeze was passed by the Senate. Critics of arms control complained that the various agreements had failed to address the most important strategic problems of the United States, in particular the vulnerability to preemptive attack of American land-based missiles. Both supporters and critics were disappointed that arms control had done little to reduce the world's stockpiles of nuclear weapons. The point received emphasis in the Reagan administration's decision to change the name of the negotiations from SALT, the acronym for strategic arms *limitation* talks, to START, for strategic arms *reduction* talks.

The debate bespoke disillusionment with what two decades of serious, sustained negotiation on nuclear weapons had accomplished. Whether similar disenchantment is present within the ranks of the relevant Soviet officials is unknown. Even if the flagging of enthusiasm is confined to the United States, it weakens support for continuing negotiations and further agreements. Still, there are reasons to expect that despite the doubts that arose in the second half of the 1970s and the divisions within the American nuclear community, modest negotiated agreements between the two superpowers will be part of the nuclear future.

The American president, whoever he may be, is likely to favor such agreements. He has a special responsibility for nuclear weapons. He is in charge of the American arsenal. If it is ever to be used, he must give the order.

The Arms Race

A military officer with a satchel containing the equipment that connects him to the thousands of bombs over which he has authority follows him everywhere, even into the hospital, as when President Reagan was shot.

This responsibility is bound to weigh heavily on the person who holds the office. It has had one particular effect on every man who was president between 1945 and 1980. Each of them, from Harry Truman to Jimmy Carter, advocated, although not always successfully, arms control agreements with the Soviet Union. Such agreements, modest though they have been, have seemed to be one way of coping with the president's singular responsibility of avoiding circumstances in which he would be obliged to give the order to fire.

Arms control agreements have military value. They impart a measure of predictability to the balance between the two superpowers. Since what each side believes it needs depends on what the other side has, the more confident each is of the other's nuclear plans, the more comfortable both can be with their own. Treaties will commend themselves to both sides as devices for managing the arms race.

They can also reduce its cost. This is perhaps the clearest benefit that the United States and the Soviet Union have drawn from the nuclear agreements that they have reached. The ABM Treaty probably averted an expensive competition in the machinery of defense. The restrictions on offensive weapons may have made the arms race somewhat cheaper for both sides than it would otherwise have been. Its cost is likely to become increasingly burdensome for both countries over the next two decades.

The enormous economic difficulties of the Soviet Union are well known. The United States faces the task of replacing the most expensive parts of its nuclear arsenal, the delivery vehicles for strategic weapons. The B-52 bomber, the Minuteman land-based missile, and the Polaris submarine were all built in the 1950s and early 1960s. Conditions will be different in the last two decades of the century. For much of the earlier period economic growth was robust; now it is feeble at best. Since then competing claims on the federal budget have arisen, in the form of the social programs that have been voted into being in the last twenty years. Other military missions, too, will compete with the building of strategic nuclear weapons systems for federal funds: increasing the firepower of NATO's nonnuclear forces in Europe; counterbalancing the growth of Soviet strength in the Western Pacific; and protecting the sea routes by which oil reaches the West from the Persian Gulf, perhaps even the oil fields themselves.

The two sides will differ in their respective capacities to sustain the arms race, but the differences may offset each other. The Soviet Union's economic condition will be far worse than that of the United States, the civilian uses for its resources much more urgent. But the Soviet government will have in the future, as it has had in the past, a political capacity to ignore other needs and build weapons that will far exceed that of its American counterpart. Each may in the end, however, find arms control agreements an attractive way of limiting their competition and thus saving money.

If the agreements of the future follow the pattern of the past, they will have an odd feature. The impulse for negotiated agreements comes from the fear of nuclear war. Preventing nuclear war was the aim of the original disarmament scheme, which gave rise to the "first step" approach, which in turn led to the negotiations that the United States and the Soviet Union have been holding for over a quarter century. Preventing nuclear war is the reason that the American president—as well, perhaps, as his Soviet counterpart—invariably has become a partisan of nuclear negotiations.

Yet the agreements that the two superpowers have concluded have had little to do with issues of war and peace. Political disputes cause war. Arms control agreements do not address them. It is true that the two nuclear giants have an overriding interest in avoiding war with each other, that to succeed they must cooperate, even if only tacitly, and that arms control provides a measure of reassurance by serving as a symbol of the possibility of cooperation. This, however, is a very modest contribution to nuclear peace. At the heart of the Soviet-American conflict lie differences in values and systems of governance, and disagreements about the political organization of Europe and indeed the world. These are issues about which, on the whole, formal agreement is not possible.

A number of measures have been proposed that do address more directly the use rather than the deployment of nuclear weapons. They are often called confidence-building measures. While an increase in mutual confidence may be a by-product of arms control agreements, it is the main goal of the "hot line," a telex link by which the American and Soviet leaders can speak directly to each other in moments of danger, and the practice of notifying the other superpower in advance of large-scale military maneuvers in Europe.

The best-known and perhaps the most controversial confidence-building measure is the promise not to be the first country to use nuclear weapons in a conflict, a promise that the Soviet Union has made but that the United States has refused to give. The idea is to raise the "nuclear threshold," to prevent the use of nuclear weapons even if war breaks out between the superpowers. The American government has declined to issue a no-first-use pledge on the grounds that the Warsaw Pact enjoys a preponderance in nonnuclear military forces in Europe, and so to rule out the possibility of repelling a Soviet attack by nuclear weapons is to concede defeat in advance. The West Europeans, and especially the West Germans, have not wanted NATO to give up the right to draw on its nuclear arsenal in response to a Soviet assault, even if that assault did not involve the use of nuclear weapons.

If the shortcoming of arms control agreements is their irrelevance to the issues on which peace depends, the drawback of confidence-building measures is their dubious effectiveness. A pledge not to initiate nuclear combat might be honored in a war, but it might not be. As long as the weapons are available there will be a chance that it will not be, and any country facing a nuclear-armed adversary would have to take that possibility into account no matter what declarations the adversary had made on the subject.

Arms control agreements are not really expected to bear directly on questions of war and peace. There is, however, a widely held expectation, or more properly a hope, that negotiations will stop and reverse the arms race between the two superpowers. It is an expectation held not just by the public at large but by members of the nuclear priesthood. Americans, Soviets, and officials of other countries all endorse substantial reductions in the two main nuclear stockpiles. The idea of reductions commands unanimous rhetorical support in the international community. It is likely to be mentioned, indeed demanded, wherever the world's diplomats gather, especially at the United Nations. Arms control agreements between now and the year 2000 are not likely, however, to reduce appreciably the American and Soviet nuclear arsenals.

Neither the United States nor the Soviet Union is likely to consider the task of reduction truly urgent. There is no necessary connection between large forces and a high danger of war. The reverse may be true. The more heavily armed each side is, the more catastrophic war will appear, and the less likely both sides will be to risk one. The more weapons each side has, moreover, the less likely any technical development will be to deprive either of the capacity for assured destruction, on which stable deterrence rests. A preemptive strike would seem to be more feasible against a few weapons than against a great many.

Large nuclear arsenals also serve a political purpose for the United States and the Soviet Union. They are a source of international privilege. Because the two are more heavily armed than other countries, they are far more powerful than any others; because they are more powerful, they are more influential. Their high force levels ensure them against the emergence of a third superpower, which would make the world more complicated and less pleasant for both. Their huge nuclear arsenals also help indirectly to discourage something that neither favors and that they have cooperated to try to prevent. An issue that draws the world's two major powers together is bound to be significant. This one, in fact, will be the second principal influence in shaping the nuclear future. It is the prospect of the spread of nuclear weapons; the prospect, that is, of nuclear proliferation.

[79]

[3]

Nuclear Proliferation

The machines that the Industrial Revolution has produced have not remained within the borders of the countries where they were first invented. They have spread elsewhere. The automobile, the steel mill, the television set, and the machines for making them are to be found all over the world.

The assortment of machines that a country has determines its prosperity. Industrialization has become the key to national wealth. Its stock of machines of war is the basis of its power. The United States and the Soviet Union are the most powerful of all countries because they are richest in the supreme machines of war—nuclear weapons.

The diffusion of nuclear weapons, like their constant improvement, has been an industrial process. Unlike the steady improvement and expansion of the American and Soviet nuclear arsenals, the spread of these weapons has proceeded at an uneven pace. The regularity of the arms race, especially since the late 1950s, makes it possible to predict with some confidence what the American and Soviet nuclear arsenals will look like in the year 2000. The technology that will be available in the near term is known now, and both sides are likely to make use of it. In regard to the distribution of nuclear armaments, the first question about the nuclear future—What will the world look like?—is much more difficult to answer. It is harder to know which countries that do not now have the bomb will get it during the next two decades.

In regard to the diffusion of nuclear weapons, the answer to the second question about the nuclear future— What difference will it make?—is, or seems to be, much clearer. The arms race may or may not give one of the superpowers or the other some advantage in their ongoing rivalry. On nuclear proliferation the nuclear priesthood, the public, and the leaders of virtually every country agree in principle: it will be bad for everybody.

The universal aversion to the spread of nuclear weapons rests on three closely related assumptions, which are widely held but seldom explicitly stated. The first is that proliferation is likely to gather momentum. The bomb is expected to spread like an infectious disease until it reaches epidemic proportions—until the whole world has become a nuclear-armed camp. A few more nuclear weapon states will lead to several more, it is thought, and several more will lead to many more. The psychology of the stampeding crowd is considered likely to take hold, as in a run on a bank when the belief spreads that the depositors will lose their money. The fear of being left out, of being left with no means of defense in a nuclear-armed world, will dominate international politics, as it did during the "scramble for Africa" among the great powers of Europe in the 1880s. At the beginning of that decade the Europeans controlled very little of the continent. Then Britain took over Egypt when the indigenous government seemed about to collapse, for fear that otherwise a colonial rival would seize it. France feared being excluded from Africa and began to establish colonies there, and Germany sought them as well. By the end of the decade much of Africa had been partitioned among the European powers, less because they prized it than because once partition seemed to be under way, all wanted to avoid being left out.

The assumption that nuclear weapons will spread around the world in this way has a certain logic. When a country gets the bomb, its neighbors will feel threatened. The obvious way for them to meet the threat is with bombs of their own. The course of nuclear proliferation since 1945 may be seen as a kind of chain reaction, with new members of the club of nuclear weapon states joining because a potential adversary belonged. The American bomb, which was produced partly out of concern that Germany was trying to make one, inspired the Soviet nuclear program; the Soviet nuclear force drove China into the nuclear business; India's nuclear explosion was a response to China's arsenal, and now Pakistan is reported to be attempting to match India's achievement. A Pakistani bomb, if there is one, will be the result, according to this interpretation, of a sequence of events that began with the Manhattan Project, which was completed before the Muslim state in South Asia was even founded.

The rapid appearance of many new nuclear arsenals is considered dangerous because it is assumed that they will make nuclear war more likely. This second assumption comes from an intuitive sense of how the law of averages works: as the number of independent centers of nuclear control increases, the chance that one of them will fight a nuclear war increases also. It comes as well from the belief that the features of the Soviet-American rivalry that have made for nuclear peace are not present elsewhere. The superpowers' political quarrel has proved manageable. Although each has wished to expand its influence, both found the distribution of territory and political dominion after World War II tolerable, or at least not so intolerable as to make war worth risking. For them the incentives for nuclear restraint have overcome the impulses for conflict. For other rivals, it is feared, the reverse might be true.

Prospective owners of the bomb are considered less reliably prudent and cautious than the superpowers. No one rash or reckless is likely to win supreme power in the United States. That statement cannot be made with the same confidence about the Soviet Union: much less is known about the way its leaders are selected, the selection has not been made often since the Communists took power in Russia in 1917, and the Soviet political system did produce Joseph Stalin. Stalin's foreign policy, at least, was relatively cautious, however. There is little reason for any confidence at all in the restraint of the leadership of many other countries. The farther the bomb spreads, therefore, the more likely it is to fall into the hands of an irresponsible or even mad national leader; that is, somebody likely to use it.

Other countries will not be able to have nuclear arsenals as large as the American and Soviet ones. The small, vulnerable nuclear forces of these other countries may tempt preemptive attacks. Even a sober leader might see some advantage in ordering one. The difference between the capacity for assured destruction and one or two bombs, it is feared, is the difference between stable deterrence and nuclear war.

[84]

It is finally assumed that the use of nuclear weapons will proceed, like their acquisition, with gathering momentum, like a chain reaction. A single nuclear shot fired in anger will lead to many more. Once broken, the taboo that has stood since Nagasaki was bombed on August 9, 1945, will disappear and the horrors of nuclear war will become commonplace.

None of these three assumptions is necessarily correct. The case can be made that all are wrong. So far the pace of proliferation has not accelerated. It has slowed. During the first decade of the nuclear age, from 1945 to 1955, three countries—the United States, the Soviet Union, and Great Britain—acquired nuclear weapons. During the next decade two followed suit—France and the People's Republic of China. Since the first Chinese explosion in 1964 there has been no full-fledged entrant into the nuclear club.

The introduction of nuclear weapons into an ongoing international conflict will not necessarily lead to nuclear war. Infant nuclear arsenals do not inevitably invite preemptive strikes. The Soviet Union has not attacked the Chinese nuclear force despite the depth of their dispute and despite rumors that an attack was being planned. (It was also rumored that the Soviets had sought American acquiescence in a preemptive attack against China.) Small nuclear arsenals are not unambiguously vulnerable. A few bombs may be hidden or moved about to make preemption appear a risky prospect. The Israeli raid on Iraq's nuclear reactor in the spring of 1981 was a preemptive strike. But the attack took place without nuclear weapons, and was directed against a reactor designed to make fissionable material, not against a stockpile of bombs. It was feasible because Iraq did not yet have any

bombs. Even if nuclear weapons do not compose interna-
tional differences, the result may not be nuclear war.
The bitterest conflicts can remain limited. The Arabs and
Israelis have fought four major wars in a quarter century.
In each of them both sides observed some restraints.

Finally, another nuclear shot fired in anger will not
necessarily lead to a barrage. The first one seems to have
had the opposite effect. The horror that Hiroshima and
Nagasaki inspired has endured long after the cities have
been rebuilt and after many thousands of other nuclear
weapons have become available, and has helped to discourage their further use.

And even if the second nuclear war should lead to a
third and fourth in rapid succession, these conflicts would
not be likely to touch off World War III. Conflicts among
other countries in which nuclear weapons were used
would threaten to draw in the superpowers, as the great
powers of Europe were drawn into war by events in
the Balkans that began with the assassination of the Aus-
trian archduke Franz Ferdinand in Sarajevo in June 1914.
But this has been true of conflicts without nuclear weapons ever since World War II. The addition of nuclear
weapons to such peripheral conflicts would make them
more dangerous, but not wholly different from those
with which the United States and the Soviet Union have
had to cope. The two have accumulated considerable experience in avoiding being drawn into direct confrontation with each other when other countries fight, and the
presence of nuclear weapons would hardly make them
less eager to stay out.

Each of the counterarguments to the reigning assumptions about the spread of nuclear weapons seems at least
plausible. None, however, commands much credence.
They are rarely even made. The world has concluded that

the consequences of nuclear proliferation will be undesirable. The uncertainty surrounding the spread of nuclear weapons promotes this conclusion. Perhaps a world of many nuclear weapon states would be as peaceful as the present world. Perhaps it would be more peaceful. But it might be considerably *less* peaceful. And if it were, it would be a very unpleasant world indeed; better to try to avoid such an eventuality. Is nuclear proliferation inevitably a bad thing? As with the question of whether a limited nuclear war is possible, the answer is uncertain, and uncertainty encourages caution, prudence, a preference for the familiar, for the existing order of things, for the status quo.

Nuclear proliferation, or rather the prevention of proliferation, is in a class with peace, prosperity, and justice; it is an issue on which everybody agrees. The consensus on the spread of nuclear weapons is all the more impressive because whereas every country is free to define the other goals as it pleases, proliferation has a specific meaning.

No country has given a nuclear weapon to another. The United States has denied such weapons even to countries that would aim them at the Soviet Union. Relatively little technical assistance useful for making a bomb has gone from one country to another. The United States worked with Great Britain during wartime, but after the war the British had to make their own nuclear weapons independently. The Soviet Union gave substantial help to the People's Republic of China in the 1950s, but had second thoughts and abruptly ended its assistance programs at the end of the decade. This was one of the causes of the rift between the two largest communist countries.

Nuclear proliferation has the status of a global problem,

one that requires international cooperation to address. The members of the international system have cooperated. They have devised a series of international rules and procedures designed to check the spread of nuclear weapons.

The centerpiece of these rules is the Nuclear Nonproliferation Treaty, or NPT, which was concluded in 1968 and went into effect in 1970. By its terms the countries with nuclear weapons promise not to help others to get them, and the countries without them pledge not to get them. By 1982, more than ninety countries had ratified the NPT.

There are some notable exceptions, including India, Israel, Pakistan, and South Africa—all potential nuclear weapon states. Two *actual* nuclear weapon states, France and the People's Republic of China, have also refused to sign the NPT. Each has denounced the treaty as ratifying international inequality, as of course it does. Neither, however, has offered nuclear assistance to any nonnuclear country, or encouraged this practice on the part of others.

In addition to the political pledges embodied in its main sections, the NPT contains technical provisions. They address the overlapping features of nuclear weapons and nuclear power plants, which can give a country a head start in getting its own bomb. The physical basis of both the fission bomb and nuclear power plants is a nuclear chain reaction, in which the splitting of one atom triggers the splitting of others. In a bomb the chain reaction builds to a crescendo and explodes. In a power plant it is steady, producing heat that vaporizes a surrounding water bath to drive steam turbines that make electricity. The fissionable material that produces the chain reaction is the same in each case, but the bomb requires the material in purer form. Both the fuel for power reactors, in most cases enriched uranium, and the by-product of the sustained chain reaction that produces electricity, plutonium, can serve as the stuff of bombs if they are rendered into purer form.

Numerous countries, including many that have signed the NPT, have nuclear power plants. To make sure that the fuel and waste from these plants are not diverted to the making of bombs, the NPT makes use of the International Atomic Energy Authority (IAEA), whose inspectors check the power plants in the nonnuclear countries that have signed the treaty to keep track of the fissionable material.

The purification of the material from a reactor so that it is suitable for a bomb (or of material found in nature so that it can be used as reactor fuel or as the basis of a bomb) requires special equipment for enriching uranium or reprocessing plutonium, which only the most advanced industrial countries manufacture. In the mid-1970s France announced plans to transfer reprocessing equipment to South Korea and Pakistan, and West Germany arranged to build a uranium enrichment plant in Brazil. The recipient countries did not have nuclear weapons, but the possibility that they might someday want some did not seem remote.

The ostensible reason for a country to get an enrichment plant or a reprocessing facility is to be able to make its own reactor fuel instead of having to depend for it on other countries. Once in possession of either, however, a country could purify fissionable material beyond the point necessary to make it fit for a reactor and thereby acquire the basis for a bomb. International commerce in the means of purifying uranium and plutonium threatened to spread the bomb without quite breaking the rules against nuclear proliferation. Those rules had to be amended. So the representatives of countries in the business of producing purification equipment began to meet, usually in London, to devise guidelines for international nuclear commerce that would not encourage the spread of nuclear weapons. They came to be known as the London Suppliers' Club.

The Nonproliferation Treaty—or rather the rules that it embodies, which were being followed before the treaty went into effect in 1970—has had some effect on the pace of nuclear proliferation. The bomb has spread slowly, much more slowly than other industrial varieties of weapons. Other inventions and other weapons have been exported. Every new owner of the bomb has had to make it almost entirely on its own.

Many sovereign states cannot do so. Many of them do not have the bomb because others will not give it to them and they cannot make it themselves. To assemble a nuclear weapon is not the most difficult of all technical undertakings. The only real "secret" of the bomb is that it is possible, a secret that was exposed in 1945. (The fusion weapon is secret in the sense that important steps in making it must be derived from complicated mathematical formulas. A fission explosive does not involve comparable difficulties.) But bomb making is not something that can be managed by a college chemistry major working with a few friends in his basement. Nor would it be easy for a small underground terrorist group.

It requires fissionable material in quantity, which is not impossible to obtain but cannot be purchased on the open market. It requires a cadre of skilled engineers and metallurgists. It requires space to assemble the device, and much more space, of course, if it is to be tested. These are requirements that only sovereign countries can readily meet.

Technical incompetence is not the only reason that countries don't have the bomb. Many do have scientists and engineers who could make one if they were given the assignment. Nuclear abstinence for many, particularly the most advanced industrial countries, is a matter of choice.

The choice is not based only, or even mainly, on considerations of international principle. When sovereign states decide what weapons to get, they give little thought to the common good, the welfare of the international system as a whole. They decide on the basis of their own interests. France and China favor nonproliferation for *others*. Where their own nuclear decisions are concerned, *their* interests have taken precedence. Their overriding concern is security. So the technically competent nonnuclear countries have chosen not to have the bomb because they do not consider it necessary, or even, on balance, useful for their security.

The main strategic purpose that nuclear weapons serve is defense through deterrence. The United States and the Soviet Union, which have the most weapons, have other goals for which military might is indispensable. Both seek to extend their influence beyond their borders, a goal that falls outside the category of defense. Both have other kinds of military might besides nuclear weapons, and in plentiful supply. No other country has quite the same aspirations as the two superpowers. Every other country, however, needs to defend itself; this requirement, after all, is the consequence of the anarchy of the international system, which is the central fact of international life. Nuclear weapons are therefore *potentially* useful for every country. Almost all have self-defense forces of some kind. Yet very few, even of those that are able to do so, have equipped those forces with nuclear weapons.

There are obviously powerful disincentives for getting the bomb, important reasons why nuclear weapons appear to make the universal task of defense harder, not easier. These reasons vary according to whether or not the country posing the threat has nuclear weapons.

If a worrisome neighbor does not have them, then defense by nonnuclear means—defense, that is, by protection rather than by deterrence—may well be possible. The neighbor would undoubtedly be more cautious if it had to confront nuclear as well as nonnuclear armaments. But it might then get nuclear weapons of its own. The resort to nuclear deterrence might start a chain reaction of proliferation. Just as each superpower is deterred from *using* the bomb by the fear that the other will do so in return, so lesser countries may be deterred from *getting* it by the fear that rivals will get it also.

The parallel is not exact. One state might still consider itself better off if both it and its neighbor had nuclear weapons than if neither had them. This would be the case if the neighbor were more powerful in nonnuclear terms. Their nuclear arsenals would be more likely to be evenly matched, at least at first. Relations between them might be more peaceful, more stable with than without nuclear weapons. But of course they might not be. Here uncertainty affects the first country's calculations. If relations became less stable with the acquisition of nuclear weapons, the result could be disastrous. Introducing these weapons of mass destruction, even a few of them, into a conflict raises the stakes, and the risks, for both sides. It will therefore generally, although not always, seem prudent to try to get along without them.

Whether or not a country is well advised to get nuclear weapons depends largely on what its neighbors would do in response. Such things are hard to gauge in advance. A prospective nuclear power may wish to hedge its bets by following a middle path between nuclear abstinence and formal entry into the club of nuclear weapon states with the production of deliverable nuclear explosives.

"Part-way" proliferation involves getting some but not all of the elements of a nuclear arsenal. India detonated a nuclear explosion in 1974 but has not, so far as is known, fabricated an actual bomb. Israel is widely believed to have a store of weapons, or to be a few simple steps away from having one. An Israeli research reactor that produces fissionable material operates outside the jurisdiction of the IAEA, and Israel certainly has the requisite scientists and engineers.

Both Israel and India get some of the benefits of having nuclear weapons. Their would-be adversaries must reckon with the possibility of nuclear punishment in reply to an attack. Neither has suffered all of the disadvantages that proliferation invites. Neither has prompted a neighbor to get the bomb, at least not yet. Part-way proliferation is a tactic for having it both ways; for making use of some of the deterrent power of nuclear armaments without driving neighboring countries into the nuclear business or incurring whatever sanctions the international community can impose for a breach of the nuclear rules.

Nuclear weapons would seem to be unambiguously attractive to nonnuclear countries that must confront one or the other of the superpowers. None could hope to defend itself by protection against either of them; none, that is, could hope to ward off the United States or the Soviet Union in nonnuclear combat if either brought the full weight of its military might to bear (as the United States did not in Indochina). Their huge nuclear arsenals make the two superpowers all the more formidable.

No lesser state could hope to match the American or Soviet nuclear forces, at least not in the short term. None could be as certain of being able to inflict devastating punishment in response to a superpower attack as the superpowers are of destroying any attacker in a second strike, including each other. Still, a few nuclear weapons in third-power hands would make an attack dramatically riskier for the superpower. Each bomb is so destructive that even a single one would do grave damage if it landed. It could kill a million people or more. It could pulverize a capital city.

A handful of bombs would give a superpower pause. It might be able to destroy all of them in a preemptive attack; but it might not. The price if it tried and failed could be extraordinarily high. Neither the United States nor the Soviet Union could be absolutely certain of crippling the entire nuclear force of a lesser nuclear power in a preemptive strike. In that uncertainty would lie a measure of safety for the lesser country.

This is the rationale for the French nuclear arsenal, and presumably also the Chinese, both of which have as their mission the deterrence of the Soviet Union. The French say that their weapons are designed to "tear an arm off the bear." This is not quite the same thing as the policy of "pure" deterrence that some prescribe for the United States. France could not be certain of mortally wounding the Soviet Union, of destroying a quarter of its population and a third of its industry, after absorbing a Soviet attack. But after such an attack enough of the French nuclear arsenal *might* survive to hit a few targets in the Soviet Union, perhaps even Moscow, even as France itself was crushed.

The chance that this would happen, the French say, can prevent a Soviet attack. Once again uncertainty is the ally of deterrence. Moreover, an attack on France would have to reckon with the French missile-bearing submarines and would risk war with the surrounding NATO countries and so with the United States.

The People's Republic of China has no submarines, only land-based missiles, and is less closely aligned with the United States. But as with France, the Soviet Union could not be absolutely certain of attacking China and escaping retaliatory punishment.

Many countries could equip themselves with enough nuclear firepower to tear an arm off the bear, or a wing off the eagle. None has followed the French and Chinese examples. One reason is that in the nuclear era the protection of territorial and political integrity has been a less urgent matter than at other periods in the history of the international system. Since 1945 they have generally been respected. More or less full sovereignty has been the international norm. There have of course been conspicuous exceptions, but the superpowers have on the whole behaved differently toward less powerful peoples than did the great European powers of the eighteenth and nineteenth centuries, who conquered much of the world beyond Europe and incorporated it into large multinational empires. The age of empire is largely although not entirely over. The impulse to acquire nuclear weapons has accordingly been weaker than it might otherwise have been.

Some countries do have well-founded fears of superpower intervention. Some play unwilling host to one of them, but cannot, for technical or political reasons, or both, get the bomb to defend themselves. A multinational empire of sorts does, after all, hold sway in Eastern Europe and Central Asia, but the nations that are part of it have had no chance to acquire nuclear armaments. Afghanistan and Poland have the motive but not the means for nuclear proliferation.

Some countries with well-founded fears of a superpower and the technical skills and political opportunity to assemble a bomb rely for their safety on defense by deterrence, but not *nuclear* deterrence. Finland, Sweden, and Yugoslavia all have nonnuclear defense plans designed to make a Soviet invasion costly, although none could, in the end, withstand a determined Soviet attack. In these cases uncertainty is at work in two ways. It reinforces deterrence. Although none of these countries is part of NATO, each is part of Europe, where the superpowers have maneuvered gingerly. The Soviets must worry that an invasion of any of the three, despite their formal independence of either coalition, would touch off a general European war, which, according to Soviet doctrine, would be a nuclear war. Uncertainty is also a reason why these European countries have chosen nonnuclear deterrence. If they were to get nuclear weapons, the Soviets might become more cautious, but they might also become more anxious and aggressive. A Yugoslav or Swedish or Finnish nuclear arsenal could have a provocative effect. It could make each country *less* secure. The uncertainty weighs in their national deliberations on the side of caution, of the status quo, which means nuclear abstinence.

There is a final group of countries that could but don't have nuclear weapons. Theirs is the most important nonnuclear category because it includes large, wealthy states that could easily equip themselves with many nuclear weapons and that have an incentive to do so, since they are plainly threatened by the Soviet Union. These countries do depend for their defense on nuclear deterrence, but it is the nuclear weapons of *another* country on which they rely. The European members of NATO, Canada, and Japan all depend on the *American* nuclear arsenal. The American system of alliances is therefore an important bulwark against the spread of nuclear weapons.

The future of nuclear proliferation will depend on how strong the barriers to the spread of nuclear weapons remain. It will depend, that is, on the amount of fissionable material the world produces, on the number of inspectors the IAEA employs and the powers they have, and especially on the number of countries that come to have enough people with nuclear expertise so that international barriers cannot interfere with their nuclear plans. The future of proliferation will depend as well on the incentives to get the bomb; on how threatened the various technically eligible countries feel, how they evaluate the likely impact of a nuclear arsenal on the threats that they face, and how much faith they place in their allies' promises to defend them.

All this adds up not to a prediction or a formula, but to a laundry list. About this part of the nuclear future, however, it is not possible to be more precise. The distribution of the bomb in the year 2000 will be the result of individual decisions by the relevant countries. The study of nuclear proliferation must be the study of their various foreign and defense policies. None of these decisions is likely to be simple; each will differ from all the others. There is no way to know in advance how any of these decisions, let alone all of them, will come out. There is no theory of how nations decide whether or not to join the nuclear club.

The case of Pakistan illustrates the difficulties of predicting the nuclear future. After India's 1974 nuclear explosion the Pakistani president, Zulfiqar Ali Bhutto, vowed that his country would get the bomb even if its people had to "eat grass" to be able to afford it, and since then a major effort to acquire nuclear weapons seems to have been under way. Reports have since appeared that Pakistan has acquired relevant technology from Europe illicitly. Bhutto, however, has been deposed and executed. His successor, General Mohammed Zia ul-Haq, has asserted, in vague terms, that his country's nuclear programs have only peaceful purposes. Getting the bomb might in fact make Pakistan less, not more secure. It might cause India to make usable weapons. Pakistan's currently cordial relations with another neighbor, the People's Republic of China, might turn sour.

Pakistan also has a border with Afghanistan, which the Soviet Union has partially occupied since 1979. Several hundred thousand Afghan refugees have crossed that border. The Afghan resistance has its base in the refugee camps and uses them as staging areas for military operations against the Soviets. Pakistani relations with the Soviet Union are uneasy at best. Nuclear weapons would complicate and perhaps dramatically worsen them.

In response to the Soviet occupation of Afghanistan, the United States has provided substantial military assistance to Pakistan. Sentiment against nuclear proliferation runs deep in the American public. Pakistan would therefore risk forfeiting that assistance if it got the bomb. It could thereby invite the worst of both worlds, infuriating a powerful enemy while alienating the only available friend of comparable strength. Pakistan might hedge its bets with some form of part-way proliferation, but that step might invite international animosity without the offsetting military advantages of a full-fledged nuclear arsenal.

Anticipating Pakistan's nuclear future is even more difficult because it will not depend solely on considerations of national security; that is, on Pakistan's relations with other countries. A bomb can provide an infusion of national pride. It may appear as the hallmark of a modern, robust, self-confident nation. Pakistan's self-confidence has never fully recovered from the secession of its eastern wing to form the independent country of Bangladesh after India's defeat of the largely western Pakistani army in 1971. A bomb might also win esteem for Pakistan among other Muslim countries as the owner of the first "Islamic bomb."

Internal politics will also bear on the question of whether Pakistan gets the bomb. General Zia has been unwilling to surrender the authority he seized in a coup d'état but unable to consolidate his power. Presiding over the acquisition of a nuclear arsenal might appear to him to be a way of putting himself firmly in command of the country. If he were to be unseated, his successor might have the same attitude toward the bomb, or an entirely different preference for Pakistan's nuclear future. The transition of leadership in the Pakistani political system is not orderly, nor is one leader bound to follow the same broad policies as another. And whatever happens in Pakistan, there may well be national leaders elsewhere who will feel more secure and powerful at home with the bomb even if it makes their countries *less* secure abroad.

Considerations of national pride and internal politics as well as national security will influence the nuclear decisions of other countries, such as South Africa, Taiwan, Argentina, and Iraq, which are frequently mentioned as future members of the nuclear club. Such considerations have already had some bearing on the nuclear decisions of the past. France got the bomb not only out of fear of a Soviet strike but also because doing so seemed a way of keeping faith with France's legacy, and self-proclaimed destiny, as an important force in international politics. The events leading up to India's 1974 explosion are not fully known, but it is unlikely to have been strictly a response to the development of the Chinese nuclear arsenal, which had begun a decade before, a decade in which, although relations between the world's two most populous countries were not entirely cordial, there was no episode like the 1962 border war between them.

Each country's decision to get or forgo nuclear weapons will of course depend partly on what other countries do. It will depend not only on the nuclear weapon policies of each technically competent country's neighbors, but also on the nonproliferation policy of the international community as a whole.

The world has responded to proliferation in the past in two not entirely consistent ways. The political status of each new nuclear-weapon state has changed very little. The United States and the Soviet Union became political rivals independently of the nuclear-weapons program of either country. Britain and France remained allied or aligned with the United States after they acquired the bomb. The Sino-Soviet split predated the first Chinese nuclear explosion, and the United States moved to improve its relations with the People's Republic despite, not necessarily because of, the Chinese nuclear arsenal. India's nuclear explosion has had little evident impact on its relations with the rest of the world.

Yet each milestone in the history of nuclear proliferation, each unexpected or unsettling addition to the club of nuclear-weapon states, has inspired an effort to keep other countries from following suit. Each has provoked efforts to raise the barriers and tighten the rules against proliferation.

The first episode in the history of nuclear proliferation, the American bombing of Hiroshima and Nagasaki, gave rise to the Baruch Plan, which was intended to prevent the further spread of the bomb by putting all aspects of atomic energy under international control. It was never implemented. It failed because, although one of the superpowers, the United States, devised and sponsored it, the other, the Soviet Union, was opposed.

No nonproliferation measure has a chance of success without at least the tacit support of both superpowers. Neither has been willing to discipline or ostracize new nuclear-weapon states in order to discourage the further spread of the bomb. Neither has been willing to put nonproliferation at the center of its foreign policy. But both *have* supported measures general enough so as not to interfere directly with their relations with particular countries.

In response to the French and Chinese nuclear explosions, they worked out the terms of the NPT and then coaxed and pressured other countries to sign it. The In-

dian explosion of 1974 and the prospective sale of uranium enrichment and plutonium reprocessing facilities
to nations considered prone to proliferation led to a tight-
ening of the procedures for exporting nuclear weapon-
related material in the United States, to the formation of
the London Suppliers Club, and ultimately to the International Nuclear Fuel Cycle Evaluation Conference, a
series of meetings to reconsider nuclear energy and its
relationship to nuclear weapons.

The next unanticipated or troubling nuclear event may
be expected to have a comparable effect. Its effect will
be all the greater if it is not an addition to the nuclear
club but the use of nuclear weapons by one or more of
the countries that already have them. The second nuclear
war is bound to shock the world. The consequences of
that shock are difficult to predict. But it will surely en-
gage the energies of the third broad source of influence
over the nuclear future, the one of most recent origin
and of least certain impact, Western public opinion.

[4]

The Anti–Nuclear Weapons Movements

Of all modern machines, indeed of all the artifacts of modern culture, the bomb is the most frightening. It is the most dangerous of all human inventions. The American, European, and Soviet people have always known how dangerous it is. They have, nevertheless, left nuclear weapons in the hands of the nuclear priesthood. (In the Soviet Union this has not been a matter of choice.) In the 1980s some in the West resolved to take control of the bomb. They began to demand that disarmament replace deterrence as the principal nuclear business of the Atlantic alliance.

Probably from 1945 onward the average American or European would, if asked, have said that he wanted to do away with all nuclear arsenals rather than refine or increase them. But the average Westerner was not asked, and did not say so, at least not in any way that influenced public policy. In the 1980s citizens of the West did begin to say so, publicly, loudly, and in growing numbers. For the first time, a mass movement dedicated to shaping the nuclear future appeared on both sides of the Atlantic.

In this, as in other things, the North American and the

European wings of NATO differ. Opposition to the alliance's nuclear weapons policies made itself known earlier in Europe than in the United States. Both European
and American anti–nuclear weapons activists aimed ultimately to lift the nuclear siege that the world must endure as long as these weapons exist. But each rallied
around a more immediate issue, and the issues were different. The Europeans opposed the stationing of 572 intermediate-range missiles on the continent, which the
NATO governments deemed necessary to offset comparable Soviet weapons. In the United States a proposal to
freeze the deployment, testing, and manufacture of all
weapons by both superpowers attracted wide support.
Since they began at different times, under different circumstances, for different (as well as for some of the same)
reasons, the European and North American anti–nuclear
weapons movements may be expected to have different
futures.

The American movement carries the stamp of political
respectability and so the potential for political influence.
The core of the movement is made up of professional and
religious groups. The most prominent of them, the Phy-
sicians for Social Responsibility, was founded to inform
people of the catastrophic medical consequences of nuclear war. Lawyers and other professionals also organized themselves to lobby on nuclear weapons issues.
The Catholic clergy began to speak out against the arms
race, and the American Conference of Bishops drafted a
pastoral letter that condemned the use of nuclear weapons against civilian targets and the initiation of nuclear
war, and called for progress in arms reduction. The Protestant National Council of Churches also took up the
nuclear question. The efforts of these groups put the nu-

clear future on the public agenda in the United States. These organizations were among the sponsors of the lectures, rallies, and marches that took place in the spring of 1982.

The fear about the nuclear future that created some of these groups and turned the attention of others to nuclear issues seemed to arise suddenly, like an abrupt, unexpected change in the weather. In fact, a current of anxiety about the bomb has always been present in the collective American psyche but has seldom affected public affairs. The nation's nerve of sensitivity to nuclear weapons issues has by and large lain buried, insulated. Every so often, however, something has touched it.

The first Soviet nuclear explosion alarmed Americans, many of whom had assumed that the Soviets would need several decades to master the techniques of bomb making. The launch in 1957 of Sputnik, the first earth-orbiting satellite, was even more alarming because the Soviets appeared to be not just catching up, as in 1949, but surpassing the United States in a crucial area of technical and military rivalry. Sputnik turned the public conversation in the United States into an exercise in national soul-searching. Americans worried about how their country compared with the Soviet Union in everything from steel production to the reading abilities of six-year-olds. Out of this self-examination came, among other things, an increased emphasis on teaching and research in science.

During the Berlin crisis of 1961 President Kennedy announced plans for every American to have access to a fallout shelter. His announcement touched off a mild wave of panic. A rush to build and stock private shelters began, as did discussions about the obligations of those who owned private shelters to neighbors who were imprudent enough to be without them in the event of a nuclear attack.

In the late 1960s plans to construct ballistic missile defense systems for American cities aroused public opposition, even from those who were supposed to be protected. The Nixon administration changed the purpose of the ABM system it was proposing from the protection of cities to the defense of missiles, thus making the program consistent with a policy of deterrence through assured destruction. Ultimately it signed the ABM Treaty.

Ten years later the citizens of Utah and Nevada made it clear that they were not willing to play host to the MX missile, which was to be based in a sprawling network of interconnected shelters. They were leery of the effect that its construction would have on the desert, the water supply, and the way of life of the small towns near the site. Nor were they eager to live next to what was sure to be a target of any Soviet attack.

In each case an issue having to do with nuclear weapons provoked a public reaction in the United States, although none inspired a genuine mass movement. The episodes had two important features. The first Soviet nuclear explosion, Sputnik, the Cuban missile crisis, and the Berlin crisis all made war seem imminent, or at least much more likely than before. And all of them forced Americans to think about what they prefer, and ordinarily manage, to ignore: the nuclear peril in which we all live. Each episode made explicit what is universally understood but usually kept buried in a distant corner of people's minds: that nuclear war, a war of annihilation, is technically possible. Both superpowers are well prepared to fight one. Fallout shelters and systems of ballistic missile defense were to be placed in or near cities where millions of people would see them every day, rather than in such sparsely populated parts of the country as North Dakota, the home of the Minuteman missile, or beneath the seas, like the nuclear-armed submarines. They were not going to be out of sight, and so would be hard to put out of mind.

The Reagan administration's nuclear weapons policies during its first fifteen months in office also reminded Americans that they lived in the shadow of the bomb, and made the nuclear peace seem precarious. The Reagan policies suggested if not a taste for war, at least a certain carelessness about the dangers of the nuclear age. The president himself carried the burden of lingering doubts about his commitment to nuclear peace, the legacy of the occasionally bellicose rhetoric that marked his political career and particularly the 1976 presidential election campaign, when his rival for the Republican nomination, then president Gerald Ford, put these doubts at the center of his own primary campaign. "Governor Reagan couldn't start a war. President Reagan could," said one of the Ford television commercials.

Ordinarily somebody whose trustworthiness on the nuclear issue is subject to public doubt cannot be elected president. This was Barry Goldwater's fate in 1964. Reagan worked hard to dispel the doubts, and succeeded well enough to win the presidency in 1980. The doubts were reawakened, however, by his administration's rejection of SALT II and its delay in resuming nuclear negotiations with the Soviets, its public discussion of the possibility of fighting and winning a nuclear war, its renewed emphasis on civil defense, and the public disagreement between the secretaries of state and defense about whether NATO plans called for the firing of a nuclear "warning shot" in response to a Soviet attack in Europe. Any one of these events by itself might have been taken more or less in stride. Together, in combination with previous suspicions about the president, they struck the public's nuclear nerve.

For the first time the public response took the form of a political movement, in part no doubt because of the power of example of the political movements of the recent past. There is an instructive similarity between the organized protest against American nuclear weapons policy and a movement that is in most ways quite dissimilar —the movement for a constitutional amendment to require a balanced federal budget. Both movements were begun outside Washington by people without professional political credentials. Both gained sufficient support at the grass roots to encourage national political leaders to attach themselves to the causes that they represent. Elected officials of all political stripes have professed allegiance to the principle that each movement seeks to promote—nuclear and fiscal restraint—but have contended that the specific measure that each movement has adopted to achieve its commonly sought goal is too restrictive, and if enacted would subvert rather than help to achieve that goal. Freezing both nuclear arsenals, it is said, would eliminate any Soviet incentive to negotiate arms control agreements and would compel the United States to keep obsolete, dangerous weapons while forgoing newer, safer ones. Similarly, it is argued, a rigid commitment to a balanced budget would prevent the necessary adjustments of federal fiscal policy to changing economic conditions.

One of the purposes of each movement, however, is precisely to tie the hands of public officials. Without statutory limits on their freedom of maneuver, partisans of both the nuclear freeze and the balanced budget amendment believe, political leaders will *not* exercise nuclear or fiscal restraint no matter what they say. The two movements therefore draw on distrust of public officials, which has grown dramatically in the United States since the mid-1960s.

The anti–nuclear weapons movement has struck two responsive chords in American public opinion: anxiety about the bomb and distrust of the government. The first has been part, although not usually a visible part, of American life since 1945; the second is perhaps the most significant development in the nation's attitudes toward public affairs in the last two decades. This suggests that the movement has deep roots in American society, and is thus likely to grow in numbers and influence.

The movement against nuclear weapons is closer in spirit, in tactics, and in goals to several other recent political movements, however, and comparisons with those movements suggest that it is *not* likely to affect the nuclear future. One of the strengths of the civil rights movement, for instance, was the fact that its central issue could not be kept out of sight and out of mind. By the 1960s black Americans were no longer willing to accept discrimination. They were determined to press their claim for equality until the nation honored it. By contrast, Americans have normally ignored the nuclear peril. Each episode of public anxiety about the bomb has given way to longer periods in which nuclear weapons issues were the preoccupation of the nuclear specialists alone. There is another telling difference between the two movements. The goal of the civil rights movement lay within the power of the United States, and the United States alone, to achieve.

The anti–nuclear weapons movement will have to win over governments its members do not elect.

This is a point on which the anti–nuclear weapons movement also differs from both organized protest against the Vietnam war and the nearest thing to an American mass movement against the bomb before the 1980s, the campaign in the late 1950s and early 1960s to put an end to nuclear testing. The antiwar movement wanted to stop the fighting in Vietnam, or at least active American participation in it. Eventually United States combat forces did withdraw from Southeast Asia, and later the war ended entirely. Americans and others wanted an end to nuclear tests because scientific evidence indicated that the radioactivity they deposited in the atmosphere caused cancer. The 1963 treaty did stop the contamination of the environment, although it did not stop nuclear testing, which continued underground.

Total disarmament, for the anti–nuclear weapons movement the equivalent of the end of the Vietnam war and the prohibition of poisonous nuclear explosions, is not feasible. Because it is not feasible, the movement will have difficulty in sustaining the interest and enthusiasm of its members and in recruiting new ones. The rate of enlistment in a hopeless cause is ordinarily low. It is, in any event, taxing to keep the mind fixed on the dangers of annihilation. It is not surprising that most people prefer to leave the subject to the nuclear experts.

A large anti–nuclear weapons movement could help to promote arms control agreements. Had the groundswell of concern about nuclear issues appeared two or three years earlier, it might have affected the fate of SALT II. But measures like the SALT treaty are probably too modest and too complicated to serve as banners around which a mass movement can rally. It is hard to imagine people giving time and money and taking to the streets on behalf of a document so long and involved that only a few officials fully understand it, and one that leaves both the United States and the Soviet Union extraordinarily heavily armed even after all the terms are fulfilled. It is hard, therefore, to imagine the American anti–nuclear weapons movement playing a major role in the nuclear future.

The Western Europeans shared the American nervousness about the nuclear weapons policies of the Reagan administration; this anxiety partly accounts for the rise of an anti–nuclear weapons movement on the other side of the Atlantic. The nuclear policies of Mr. Reagan's predecessor also agitated the European members of NATO. Jimmy Carter's proposal to deploy the enhanced radiation warhead, commonly known as the neutron bomb—a nuclear weapon whose main destructive effect is radiation rather than blast or heat and is designed for use against the large tank formations of the Warsaw Pact—caused particular dismay. In fact, American nuclear policy well before the Carter administration distressed the Europeans. Their discontent spans two decades. It has arisen less from a lack of confidence in any particular president than from a basic disagreement with the United States about deterrence in Europe.

The reigning American view since the early 1960s has been based on the idea of escalation dominance, which presumes the possibility of warfare between the superpowers less severe than the nuclear destruction of cities, and so prescribes military forces suitable for fighting at these lower levels. The Europeans have had a different view. They have believed that successful deterrence depends on the conviction of the Soviet leaders that *any* war in Europe would *inevitably* become all-out nuclear war. They have resisted a declaration that NATO could wage war at various rungs on the escalation ladder.

The reason for the European view is not quite the same as the reason that some Americans have considered the simple capacity for assured destruction to be adequate to deter the Soviet Union. The champions of pure deterrence believe that the possibility of full-scale war is sufficiently alarming to keep wars from breaking out at lesser levels of violence. The Europeans have feared that lesser wars might in fact break out. They have not wished to fight them. They have not wished to fight wars of *any* kind. World War III, even if it spared American cities, even if it did not involve the use of nuclear weapons, would be catastrophic for the inhabitants of the countries where it would be fought, or so they have believed. World War II was enough for the Europeans.

They have feared that if the West were ready to fight World War III in some "limited" fashion, the Soviet Union would oblige. Making war more feasible by making it less catastrophically destructive, they have feared, would make it more likely. They objected to the neutron bomb because it was designed for a nuclear war confined to the battlefields of Central Europe. They were unhappy with the prospect of new intermediate-range nuclear forces because those weapons could, in theory, be used in a war that would spare North America. Both weapons, that is, had as their missions war between the two military blocs at levels below mutual annihilation. And while the government of the United States has consistently believed that deterrence in Europe depended on NATO's visible readiness to fight at levels below all-out nuclear combat, most Europeans have remained convinced that their safety required that the West appear uninterested in fighting any war other than an annihilating nuclear one.

American proponents of pure deterrence have regarded a relatively small number of nuclear weapons as sufficient to protect Europe; the advocates of escalation dominance have wanted larger and more varied forces, and on the whole have had their way. While the Europeans' *idea* of deterrence has been closer to assured destruction and pure deterrence, their preferences for the *size* and *shape* of NATO's forces have been closer to those implied by escalation dominance. The reason for this preference is another persistent European fear, which is in fact inherent in any alliance: the fear of abandonment.

The Europeans have worried that in the event of a Soviet attack the United States would not come to their rescue, especially since to do so could trigger a nuclear assault on the continental United States. They wanted American arms and especially American troops in Europe as a sign of good faith, a symbol of the strength of the American commitment to defend them. They regarded the American forces as hostages of a sort, as a kind of trip wire ready to propel the United States into a European war. Before World War I a French officer was asked how many British soldiers he wanted stationed in his country to make certain that Britain would fight at France's side against Germany. Only one, the Frenchman is reported to have replied, as long as he was certain of being killed in the first hour of the war. The Europeans have taken a similar view of American troops and American nuclear weapons.

They have wanted more than one of each. The preferred number has always turned out to be the number already there, no more and no less. More forces, the Europeans have thought, would suggest that they might actually be used in a war that would be less than catastrophic, at least for the superpowers. Fewer would suggest a weakening of the American commitment to their defense. The forces were in place for symbolic purposes. The withdrawal of some of them would be the wrong symbol. The differences between the American and the European approaches to deterrence have periodically caused friction between the two wings of the Atlantic alliance. Often, however, the allies have been able to agree on the forces to have in Europe while disagreeing on the reasons to have them there. The Americans have wanted them for resisting Soviet attacks of various kinds, the Europeans for making visible the American promise to protect them. This ongoing disagreement, moreover, has been between governments. There was as little interest in matters of strategic doctrine outside the small circle of nuclear experts in Europe as in the United States for most of the nuclear age.

The nuclear issues of the 1980s, however, engaged popular passions. They divided the public from the experts in Europe as in the United States. In late 1979 the Western European governments agreed to receive American intermediate-range nuclear weapons. They specified at the same time that negotiations to limit or reduce them had to begin, making this a condition of acceptance to placate public opposition to the weapons, which was already building.

Another danger inherent in any alliance alarmed the European public, the danger of entrapment. Every ally must worry not only that its alliance will not work, and that it will be abandoned in its hour of need, but that the alliance will work too well, dragging it into an ally's war that it has no wish to fight. What seemed to the

Reagan administration a properly firm policy toward the Soviet Union appeared to the Europeans dangerously belligerent and needlessly provocative. The average European, like the average American, may not be well versed in the nuances of deterrence theory, but he knows what he does not want. He does not want war.

The difference between the two wings of the Atlantic alliance about the proper policy toward the country that NATO was created to resist arose from differing evaluations of the policy of relaxing tensions and concluding agreements with the Soviet Union, the policy that the West followed for much of the 1970s, the policy known as détente.

From the European point of view the policy was successful. The volume of trade between the two halves of Europe grew. So did the flow of information and the number of visitors between East and West. Most important of all, the threat of war on the continent receded. The decade of the 1960s, especially its early years, had been nerve-racking; the 1970s were much more tranquil.

The Americans came to the opposite conclusion about détente. Trade with the Eastern bloc, with the exception of grain sales, remained modest for the United States. While the Europeans were reassured by the USSR's restraint on the continent, the Americans grew alarmed by the Soviets' efforts to spread their influence through the armies of allies and clients in the Middle East and in Africa. The invasion of Afghanistan and the suppression of Solidarity, the Polish trade-union movement, outraged the American public. Détente was popular in Europe; the American resolve to discontinue it therefore was not, and its unpopularity fed the discontent with the United States' nuclear weapons policies.

NATO's nuclear weapons policies provoked public protest in Europe in the 1980s for a final reason. For the first time European governments shared responsibility for deciding those policies. In the past the nuclear weapons on the continent had been put there by the American government, with the tacit consent of its European counterparts. The United States was the chief proponent of the plan for 572 Pershing missiles and ground-launched cruise missiles in 1979, but the Europeans had to vote to approve it. This arrangement invited the opinion of the European public, which turned out to be less than wholly enthusiastic about the scheme.

To refer to a single European attitude toward Western nuclear weapons policy, as toward any issue of consequence, is of course misleading. The Western part of the continent is hardly single-minded. Organized protest against nuclear weapons seemed much more extensive in the Protestant north than in the Catholic south. (This regional variation can perhaps be traced to differences of theology, the Protestant teaching that man's duty is to recreate God's kingdom on earth giving rise to a political tradition distinct from the one fostered by the Catholic emphasis on preparation for the next world.)

Of all Western European countries, the Federal Republic of Germany has most reason to worry about the nuclear future. It is the likely battleground if war occurs. It is part of a country divided between the two blocs. Détente, with its easing of obstacles to trade, travel, and communication between the two German states, is necessary for the closest approximation of a normal national existence available to the Germans. It is a country whose terrible past has produced a postwar generation in search of a national identity, a generation that is drawn to the idea of Germany as the vanguard of a movement to rid the world of nuclear weapons.

The Anti–Nuclear Weapons Movements

Great Britain, the other large European country where an organized anti–nuclear weapons movement has flourished, is the one place where such a movement existed before the 1980s. The British Campaign for Nuclear Disarmament of the 1950s and early 1960s was part of a tradition of protest going back to organized opposition to imperialism, the Corn Laws, and the slave trade.

Opposition to NATO's nuclear weapons policies is compatible with the general outlook and some specific positions of a number of parties on the political left in Europe. The left wing of the Labour party supplied much of the energy of the British movement, and in Germany the left of the Social Democratic party has been active in the anti–nuclear weapons cause.

The related but more general goal of a nuclear-free Europe has had some standing, at one time or another, with a number of left-wing parties in the southern part of the continent: the Italian Communists, Andreas Papandreou's Greek Socialists, and even the French Socialists in the days before François Mitterand became president of the Republic. This goal appeals to the European left on several counts. It is a way of opposing the United States without embracing the Soviet Union. It promises the diversion of resources from military to social programs, an important item on the left's political agenda. It is consistent with the left's reformist impulse, a program for peace abroad that corresponds to the commitment to social justice at home.

Because it is part of left-wing politics in Europe, the anti–nuclear weapons movement is likely to prove more enduring there than in the United States. It is likely to endure as well because opposition to NATO's nuclear weapons policy is related to a larger aim, which is sometimes specifically invoked. Stopping the deployment of

[117]

intermediate-range nuclear weapons is considered by some to be the first step toward the dissolution of both military blocs; the second is the removal of all nuclear weapons from the continent. Behind the European anti– nuclear weapons movement stands, among other things, the wish to escape from the control of the two partly European superpowers, and to restore the freedom of maneuver in foreign policy that the Western Europeans lost in 1945.

It is an understandable wish. The aspiration to independence is universal in the international system. No country will feel wholly comfortable while its fate rests in the hands of others, although many countries have no choice in the matter. It is a wish that can be partly fulfilled. The Soviet bloc is not about to dissolve, not as long as the Communist party of the Soviet Union has the power to prevent its dissolution, and that seems likely to be a very long time. The Western alliance, however, is voluntary. It is not immune to change, including the sort of change sometimes implied by the European anti– nuclear weapons movements.

It is in one sense surprising that such a change has not already occurred. The Atlantic alliance began as a guarantee pact, not the integrated military force that is stationed on the continent today. The United States promised to help the Europeans in the event of a Soviet attack. It was thought, however, that the Europeans would assume most of the responsibility for defending themselves once they had regained economic health. The restoration of their economic well-being was the aim of American policy from 1947 to 1950. With the outbreak of the Korean war, American troops were dispatched to Europe for a stay of indefinite duration and NATO was transformed.

Western Europe has, of course, long since recovered from the ravages of World War II, but continues to depend heavily on the United States for its defense.

It need not do so. The nations of Western Europe have the resources to defend themselves without American troops, even without an American guarantee. If they should assume the full burden of their own defense, they would free themselves from American tutelage. Their fate would no longer be tied to that of the United States. They would be able to conduct independent foreign policies. But they would probably have to sacrifice the central aim of the anti–nuclear weapons movement to achieve this independence.

Those in the European anti–nuclear weapons movement who seek complete independence from the superpowers envision a continent, or at least the western part of it, with the political character of Switzerland, Sweden, and Austria—each of them democratic, prosperous, and neutral (although the Swedes buttress their neutrality with sizable armed forces). If all of Western Europe were as small as Austria, or as distant from the great powers as Australia, this outcome might be possible. Geography and demography, however, make it highly unlikely.

In international politics, as elsewhere, power abhors a vacuum. Separation from the United States and the demilitarization of Western Europe would create a large vacuum of power in one of the richest parts of the world. Western Europe is a great strategic prize. The Soviet Union would have difficulty resisting the temptation to seize it, or at least to try to exert controlling influence over it. The Europeans would in all likelihood resent and resist such Soviet efforts. Their means of resistance would be weapons, ultimately the acquisition of nuclear weapons. So a severance of the American connection would probably mean *more* European weapons, not fewer. It would probably mean that nuclear weapons would be more widely distributed in Europe than they are at present. Without American nuclear protection it is likely that the countries of Western Europe that do not now have them, notably the Federal Republic of Germany, would follow the French example and get them.

This is a nuclear future in which the world would look different from the way it does now. Once the Western Europeans got the bomb, others—the Japanese, for instance—might decide to follow suit. The superpowers would certainly recalculate their nuclear requirements. The United States might feel secure with less nuclear firepower. The Soviet Union would almost certainly want more. It is hard to know what difference these developments would make for international politics. They might make no difference at all. The nuclear peace that has been in effect since 1945 might hold. Or it might not; the world might become radically more dangerous, chaotic, and bloody.

For this reason the future envisioned in this scenario is not likely. Uncertainty about the consequences of the disengagement of the United States from Europe works against it on both sides of the Atlantic, just as it helps to inhibit nuclear proliferation. It is in fact a future characterized by proliferation.

But it is certainly a possible future. It is the radically different set of nuclear arrangements, the sharp departure from the course that the world has followed since 1945, that is feasible. It is a future that, unlike a world without any nuclear weapons at all, the citizens of the West have it within their power to create.

[5]

The Nuclear Future Revisited

The message of this book is that the nuclear future will be like the past. It will follow a middle path between nuclear war and nuclear disarmament. There will continue to be nuclear weapons, but they will not be used, at least not by the two most heavily armed countries against each other. The superpowers will continue to deter each other. Their rivalry will continue, but will be confined to politics, to the arms race, and to proxy wars, as it has been since 1945.

The reasons that all this was true in the past will hold for the future. They may be simply summarized: the alternatives, disarmament and war, are either too difficult to achieve or too terrible to risk.

The message is that the bomb is a disease that is incurable but not fatal. As long as the world recognizes the illness and takes the proper precautions, it can continue to lead a normal life.

This is what most of the nuclear priesthood believes. This belief is the basis of the nuclear weapons policies of the West, and probably also of the Soviet Union. Those who have made these weapons their business regard them with the dispassion of the doctor, not the anxiety and horror of the patient.

But the message of the anti–nuclear weapons movement is that the experts' opinion, on which the various national nuclear weapons policies are based, is both too optimistic and too pessimistic. It is too optimistic about the sturdiness of nuclear peace. The world has enjoyed long periods of peace before. From the final defeat of Napoleon in 1815 to the outbreak of World War I in 1914 there was no major war; all international conflicts were limited. But after a century of peace a big war did come. It has always come eventually. No peace so far has lasted forever; neither will the nuclear peace.

On the other hand, the anti–nuclear weapons movements have been saying, the nuclear experts are too pessimistic about the chances for a world without nuclear weapons. No doubt such a world will require sweeping, revolutionary change. No doubt it will mean doing away with the present international system by abolishing sovereignty. Sovereignty is very old. It is not, however, immutable. It is not etched in the genes of the species *Homo sapiens*. Disarmament will be difficult but not impossible to achieve. The prospective difficulty is all the more reason to begin now to work for it.

To these objections there is no satisfactory answer. As long as there are nuclear weapons, the possibility of nuclear war cannot be reduced to zero. If there are nuclear weapons, they can be used. If they are used, the consequences can be catastrophic beyond precedent, perhaps beyond imagining. Perhaps no catastrophic nuclear war at all will take place between now and the year 2000. But reaching the year 2000 without disaster only qualifies the world to try to continue to coexist with the bomb thereafter. It is one thing to be sanguine about the chance that the nuclear peace will endure to the year 2000, quite another to be confident about the year 3000.

[122]

The Nuclear Future Revisited

What can be said about the objections of the anti–nuclear weapons movements to the nuclear orthodoxy is that one of their basic points is true. Nothing lasts forever. The lives of individuals are short. The life of the planet and that of the species, although finite, are very long. The lives of institutions, customs, and social arrangements such as those that govern nuclear weapons fall somewhere in between.

In the perspective of the 2,500-year recorded history of international politics, a transformation of the present international system, of the machines, beliefs, and rules that have kept the nuclear peace since 1945, would be revolutionary. Compared with the history of the last 25,000 years, it appears more nearly normal. In that period human beings shifted from scattered lands of hunters and gatherers to settled communities of farmers and, very recently, to producers of machines jammed together in cities. By the year 3000, or 30,000, social life may be as radically different from what it is at present as the present is from our distant nomadic past. In that case the world's nuclear arrangements may well bear little resemblance to the curent ones.

The middle way for nuclear weapons, the path between disarmament and destruction, stretches into the medium-term future. Beyond that middle distance the mind's eye cannot see. Beyond that point predictions are the products of intuition about human nature and the course of human history, of pure imagination, and of faith. For visions of the long-term nuclear future, as with all the deepest secrets of human existence, we must turn to literature and to religion, not to political analysis.

Glossary

ABM: antiballistic missile system, to protect cities against ballistic missile attack; largely prohibited by the 1972 U.S.-Soviet ABM Treaty.

ASW: antisubmarine warfare.

anarchy: the absence of government; in international politics, the fact that there is no world government.

arms control: limited agreements to restrict but not to abolish nuclear weapons.

assured destruction: the capacity to destroy a large fraction of another country's population and industry even after absorbing a nuclear attack.

ballistic missile: a missile that moves freely during most of its flight, influenced only by gravity; most are based on land or carried by oceangoing submarines.

command and control: the communications networks that link national leaders with their nuclear arsenals.

confidence-building measures: measures that give the United States and the Soviet Union confidence that the other is not planning to attack, such as prior notification of missile tests and military training maneuvers.

counterforce: attacks aimed at military facilities.

countervalue: attacks aimed at civilian populations and industry.

cruise missile: small pilotless aircraft capable of carrying nuclear weapons.

deterrence: the attempt by one party to keep another from doing something by threatening punishment in return; a central purpose of nuclear weapons.

disarmament: the abolition of all weapons; sometimes called "general and complete disarmament."

escalation: the act of raising a conflict to a more destructive level of violence.

escalation dominance: the idea that superiority in a particular category of weaponry will confer a political advantage on the United States or the Soviet Union.

flexible response: the strategy of being able to fight at different levels of force with a variety of weapons.

fusion: the process of fusing atoms together; the basis of most existing nuclear weapons, sometimes called "hydrogen bombs."

IAEA: International Atomic Energy Agency, which monitors the nuclear power plants of countries that have signed the Nonproliferation Treaty and do not have nuclear weapons to make sure that no nuclear material is being diverted to make bombs.

intermediate-range weapons: nuclear weapons based in Western Europe and aimed at the Soviet Union and based in the Soviet Union and aimed at Western Europe; sometimes abbreviated as INF (for "intermediate nuclear forces") or TNF (for "theater nuclear forces").

minimum deterrence: the idea that one country needs only to be able to inflict vast retaliatory damage on another, and not match the other weapon for weapon, in order to deter the other; sometimes called "finite" or "pure" deterrence.

mutual assured destruction: the relationship between the United States and the Soviet Union in which each can inflict grave damage on the other even after absorbing a nuclear attack.

NPT: the Nuclear Nonproliferation Treaty, a 1968 agreement by whose terms countries with nuclear weapons promise not to help others get them and countries without those weapons promise not to acquire them.

neutron bomb: a tactical nuclear weapon whose destructive effects come mainly from radiation rather than blast or heat.

SALT: Strategic Arms Limitation Talks between the United States and the Soviet Union, which produced agreements in

1972 and 1979; renamed START (Strategic Arms Reduction Talks) in 1981.

strategic weapons: nuclear weapons located within the borders of the United States and the Soviet Union or on oceangoing submarines and aimed at the other country.

tactical weapons: nuclear weapons based in Western Europe and aimed at Eastern Europe, based in Eastern Europe and aimed at Western Europe, or designated for use on a European battlefield.

throw-weight: the combined weight of all bombs and other devices carried by a single missile.

yield: the amount of energy produced by a nuclear explosion.

Selected Bibliography

The following books represent a small fraction of the many works that are available on the subject of nuclear weapons.

The History of Nuclear Weapons

Freedman, Lawrence. *The Evolution of Nuclear Strategy*. New York: St. Martin's, 1981. A very detailed account.

Lieberman, Joseph I. *The Scorpion and the Tarantula: The Struggle to Control Atomic Weapons, 1945–1949*. Boston: Houghton Mifflin, 1970. The subject is the Baruch Plan, the first American disarmament proposal.

Mandelbaum, Michael. *The Nuclear Question: The United States and Nuclear Weapons, 1946–1976*. New York: Cambridge University Press, 1979. Emphasizes the early 1960s as the formative period for strategy and arms control.

———. *The Nuclear Revolution: International Politics Before and After Hiroshima*. New York: Cambridge University Press, 1981. Compares the nuclear age with prenuclear periods.

Sherwin, Martin. *A World Destroyed: The Atomic Bomb and the Grand Alliance*. New York: Alfred A. Knopf, 1975. Emphasizes the period before Hiroshima.

The History of Arms Control

Newhouse, John. *Cold Dawn: The Story of SALT*. New York: Holt, Rinehart & Winston, 1973. Covers SALT I.

Talbott, Strobe. *Endgame: The Inside Story of SALT II.* New York: Harper & Row, 1979. The definitive book on SALT II.
Wolfe, Thomas W. *The SALT Experience.* Cambridge, Mass.: Ballinger, 1979. Covers the period between SALT I and SALT II.

Nuclear Strategy

Brodie, Bernard. *Strategy in the Missile Age.* Princeton: Princeton University Press, 1959. A classic account that remains useful.
Gompert, David C., ed. *Nuclear Weapons and World Politics.* New York: McGraw-Hill, 1977. Suggests alternative nuclear futures.
Leebaert, Derek, ed. *Soviet Military Thinking.* London and Boston: Allen & Unwin, 1981. An authoritative collection of essays on the Soviet perspective.
Legault, Albert, and George Lindsey. *The Dynamics of the Nuclear Balance.* Ithaca: Cornell University Press, 1976. Contains basic technical information.
Snyder, Glenn. *Deterrence and Defense: Toward a Theory of National Security.* Princeton: Princeton University Press, 1961. A clear statement of basic concepts.
Thompson, W. Scott, ed. *National Security in the 1980s: From Weakness to Strength.* San Francisco: Institute for Contemporary Studies, 1980. Suggests improvements for American forces.

Nuclear Proliferation

Dunn, Lewis A. *Controlling the Bomb: Nuclear Proliferation in the 1980s.* New Haven: Yale University Press, 1982. A general overview of the subject.
Potter, William C. *Nuclear Power and Nonproliferation: An Interdisciplinary Perspective.* Cambridge, Mass.: Oelgeschlager Gunn & Hain, 1981. Emphasizes the connection between nuclear weapons and nuclear power plants.
Quester, George, ed. *Nuclear Proliferation: Breaking the Chain.* Madison: University of Wisconsin Press, 1981. Good general essays.
Yager, Joseph A., ed. *Nonproliferation and U.S. Policy.* Washing-

ton, D.C.: Brookings Institution, 1980. Covers particular countries and makes policy recommendations.

Important articles on nuclear weapons are to be found in the general foreign affairs periodicals *Foreign Affairs* and *Foreign Policy*, in the more specialized *International Security*, and in *The Bulletin of the Atomic Scientists*, which was founded by people who had worked on the original program to develop these weapons.

Library of Congress Cataloging in Publication Data

Mandelbaum, Michael.
  The nuclear future.

  (Cornell studies in national security policy)
  "Original paper was published as The future of nuclear weapons in
the September-October 1982 issue of the Naval War College review"—P.
  Bibliography: p.
  1. Atomic weapons. 2. Atomic warfare. 3. Arms race—History—20th
century. I. Title. II. Series.
U264.M36   1983   355'.0217   82-74068
ISBN 0-8014-1619-1
ISBN 0-8014-9254-8 (pbk.)